THE MYTH OF DELIVERANCE

NORTHROP FRYE

The Myth
of Deliverance

REFLECTIONS ON SHAKESPEARE'S
PROBLEM COMEDIES

UNIVERSITY OF TORONTO PRESS
Toronto   Buffalo

© University of Toronto Press 1983
Toronto Buffalo London
Printed in Canada

ISBN 0-8020-6503-1

Canadian Cataloguing in Publication Data

Frye, Northrop, 1912–
The myth of deliverance : reflections on
Shakespeare's problem comedies

Based on the Tamblyn lectures, given at the University
of Western Ontario, Mar. 25–27, 1981.
ISBN 0-8020-6503-1

1. Shakespeare, William, 1564–1616 – Comedies –
Addresses, essays, lectures. I. Title. II. Series:
Tamblyn lectures ; 1981.

PR2981.F79   822.3'3   C82-095196-X

Publication of this book was made possible by grants from the
University of Western Ontario, administrator of the Tamblyn funds,
and from the Ontario Arts Council under its block grant program.

Contents

The Tamblyn Lectures, devoted to the cultivation of the humane arts and sciences, were established by John and Helen Tamblyn in memory of their parents, Dr and Mrs W.F. Tamblyn and Dr and Mrs F.K. Hughes. Their gift demonstrates the continuing commitment of the Tamblyn family to the welfare of the University of Western Ontario. The series was inaugurated in 1981 with the lectures upon which this book is based.

Preface

THIS BOOK is based on the Tamblyn lectures, given at the University of Western Ontario on 25, 26, and 27 March 1981, as the inaugural series. I am grateful to many at that university for the honour of inviting me to give the lectures and for their hospitality during my visit. I think particularly of Dean John Rowe, Professor James Reaney, and Professor John Graham, along with so many of my friends and former students who made the occasion festive.

I have written about these plays of Shakespeare before, and consequently some repetition of earlier work is inevitable; but the main course of the argument is different, and I hope the little book will suggest something of what the study of Shakespeare has invariably been for me. One begins by reading or seeing a play like other plays, subject to the conditions and limitations of its own age and to our corresponding limitations in receiving it. One ends with the sense of an exploding force in the mind that keeps destroying all the barriers of cultural prejudice that limit the response to it. In other words, we begin with a notion of what the play might reasonably be assumed to mean, and end with realizing that what the play actually does mean is so far beyond this as to be in a different world of understanding altogether.

N.F.
November 1981

1

The Reversal of Action

IN THIS BOOK I return to an interest that has preoccupied me over the years; the conception of comedy, more particularly Shakespearean comedy, and its relation to human experience. I should like to base the main argument on the three plays of Shakespeare that are sometimes called 'problem plays,' *Measure for Measure*, *All's Well that Ends Well*, and *Troilus and Cressida*. Many of the critics who first called them problem plays imposed what I consider a pseudo-problem on them which is here being ignored. The term originally suggested that these plays were more 'realistic' and more concerned with 'serious' social issues than, say, *A Midsummer Night's Dream* or *The Merry Wives of Windsor*. But while *Troilus and Cressida* is admittedly an experimental play in a special category, the other two are simply romantic comedies where the chief magical device used is the bed trick instead of enchanted forests or identical twins. Even if I cannot claim to have established the point by first-hand research, the bed trick seems to me quite as improbable as anything that goes on in the wood of Oberon and Titania – where, in fact, one of the things that does go on is the confusion of lovers' identities in the dark. There are said to be one or two actual bed tricks in history, but one suspects that drunkenness played the decisive role in them rather than darkness. In any case the bed tricks are by no means the only fantastic or incredible elements in the two plots, which, like most of Shakespeare's comedies, are essentially retellings of folk tales.

The best way to introduce my subject will be to explain, first, my chapter headings, and then my title. In a famous chapter of the *Poetics* (xi), Aristotle speaks of reversal and recognition (*peripeteia* and *anagnorisis*) as characteristic of what he calls complex plots. His distinction between simple and complex plots, and his obvious preference for the latter, seem to me connected with another distinction I have made elsewhere in discussing the structure of romance. Some romances are simply 'and then' stories, in which B follows A, and in which the reader follows both to see what happens next. But there are also 'hence' stories, in which B is presented as a credible effect of A, so that the story incorporates some sense of logic, which in a work of literature always means a special form of rhetoric.

Sometimes the effect seems to reverse the direction of the action up to that point, and when it does we are normally very close to the end. Hence a reversal in the action often forms a part of an *anagnorisis*, a word that can be translated either 'discovery' or 'recognition,' depending on how much of a surprise it is. Thus in a detective story the identifying of the murderer is a 'discovery' in the sense that we realize that he is a murderer for the first time: it is a 'recognition' in the sense that, if the normal conventions of the detective story are being preserved, he is already a well known and established character.

In a tragedy, an action that seems to be proceeding in a straight line may be, through a reversal in the action, suddenly perceived as a parabola, an action turning downward, the metaphor preserved in the word 'catastrophe.' In a comedy there is normally a reversal upward, a change from bad fortune to good, or what we might call an anastrophe. As a rule, the downward turn in tragedy appears to us as something inevitable, brought about by the will of the gods, the hero's excessive pride, or other causal agent. In comedy the upward turn of the hero's fortunes is often some kind of 'gimmick' or concealed device. Thus if a young man wants a young woman slave and can't get her, 'it turns out that' she was kidnapped by pirates in infancy and is someone respectable enough to marry. This surprising or unexpected quality in a comic structure is often so perfunctory or arbitrary that the plot seems to us simple rather than complex: first the hero is frustrated, 'and then' he's satisfied. Aristotle gives this kind of reversal a separate name (*metabasis*) and regards it as structurally inferior to *peripeteia*.

The *Poetics* is primarily concerned with tragedy, and in tragedy reversal seems deeply built into the human situation. A tragic outcome usually reverses what the hero wants, and much of the art of tragedy consists in showing that such a reversal has its own rationale. In Greek tragedy the general rule is that a hero's *hybris* or aggressive act throws out the whole machinery of law and order (*dike*), the contract of law and justice that gods, men, and nature all endorse. The conception of *nemesis* is primarily the sense of this cosmic order righting itself after it has been put out of balance by *hybris*. The pre-Socratic philosopher Anaximander even suggests that birth itself is a disturbance of nature, an aggressive act of which the *nemesis* is death. In any case *nemesis*, though its agent may be a bloodthirsty avenger or an offended god, is not merely a morally intelligible force but almost a physically intelligible one. If the hero were to get away with his aggression, the world would have to be, so to speak, recreated in the image of that aggression.

When a reversal takes place in comedy, it appeals to something in the audience that wants a happy ending for deserving characters. The audience would like to believe too that such an ending is also natural, if not inevitable. But it is very seldom that a genuinely comic resolution to a play seems the 'logical' outcome of the action. There is nearly always something residually perplexing or incredible about it. As late as *The Winter's Tale* Shakespeare is still insisting on the unlikeliness of the story he nevertheless insists on telling: 'the verity of it is in strong suspicion'; 'it would be hooted at like an old tale.' I am speaking primarily of the New Comedy form that dominated literature from later Classical times to, in England, the Victorian age. During most of that time a reader's halting perception of the naturalness of the conclusion could be assisted by assertions about the workings of divine providence in human life, providence being assumed to favour happy endings. If the belief in such a providence is not familiar enough to the audience to be incorporated into literary convention, such manufactured happy endings are often regarded as imaginatively dishonest, and a more ironic and ambiguous form of comedy takes their place.

Aristotle's terms are so suggestive that they keep spilling over all our experience of drama, including many dramatic forms and genres that Aristotle himself was not concerned with. By 'recognition' Aristotle seems to have meant primarily the recognition of some characters by other characters in the final scene. This could also be a recognition of a previously unrecognized quality in a character, of the kind we have just noted in detective stories, where we discover that one character has committed a murder. As we watch the conclusion of a play, however, we find this recognition extending from other characters to ourselves in the audience. In fact, except when the recognition is a pure surprise, the audience's recognition normally comes first. Othello's recognition of the innocence of Desdemona and the malice of Iago comes at the very end of the play, but we have recognized these things all along, and have been waiting with an almost intolerable suspense for

Othello at last to see what we see. Similarly with such comic devices as twins or concealed parentage, where the audience usually knows the essential data already. In short, reversal is primarily something the dramatist does to his plot; recognition is the response to it on the part of other characters and of the audience.

In the very concentrated Greek dramatic forms, reversal and recognition normally occur in the same place, as two aspects of the same thing, which is why Aristotle discusses them together. In the more spread-out Shakespearean tragedies there may be other reversals much earlier. In *Hamlet*, in the scene where Hamlet refrains from killing Claudius at his prayers, however we explain the scene or account for Hamlet's motivation, we realize, not simply that we are watching a tragic action – that was fairly obvious from the beginning – but that Hamlet himself is now irretrievably a doomed tragic hero. Similarly in *Antony and Cleopatra*, when Mark Antony marries Octavia. As the soothsayer has told him, Antony's evil genius is not necessarily Cleopatra, whatever the Romans may say, but Caesar; and by contracting an alliance with Caesar in this marriage he has brought the opposition of fate down on himself. When he runs after Cleopatra's galley in the battle of Actium, Antony makes a fool of himself in the ordinary colloquial sense in which we still use the word; by marrying Octavia he makes a fool of himself in a special sense largely confined to Shakespearean tragedy. That is, he becomes a victim of fate, the kind of person to whom things happen: 'fortune's fool' like Romeo, or 'the natural fool of fortune' like Lear, someone no longer in full command of his own destiny. Here the peripety comes in the middle, bending the story line downward. But it is also possible to achieve a reversal of action at the very beginning. Thus *King Lear* begins with the reversal of Lear's attempt to put on a big show of love and loyalty focused on himself, with Cordelia in the lead role.

The 'problem' comedies anticipate the romances of Shakespeare's final period in many ways: one is the very long and elaborate recognition scene, usually taking up the whole of the fifth act, in which a great number of mysteries of identity are cleared up. This elaborate recognition scene develops out of the less complex forms of it in *A Comedy of Errors* and *Twelfth Night*, where the main problem is to get the twins unscrambled. Such recognition scenes are a feature of Shakespeare's dramaturgy that a modern audience needs some historical imagination to take in – to say nothing of some critics, who often simply throw up their hands when confronted by them. For one thing, as we saw, the mysteries are usually mysteries only to the characters on the stage: the audience has already been alerted to them, and simply watches the pattern completing itself. For another, the action is as highly stylized as a puppet-play, which in some respects it resembles. Then again, the action is a disconcerting mixture of the inevitable and the incredible. The conversions, reconcilings, reunions, even resurrections, are not reflections of experience: such things happen only in plays. But they happen in these plays because they are the kind of thing that must happen if the play is to carry out its own postulates, and are inevitable structurally. Plays like this have to end like this, whatever the outrage to reality. We have next to ask why, but the answer will take us into a rather long detour.

Every society lives inside a transparent envelope known as culture or civilization, out of which the specific arts and sciences, including literature, develop. In a primitive society, whatever we may mean by primitive, it is hardly possible to separate the literary from other verbal elements of culture, but as a society grows more complex, a central, sacrosanct verbal culture emerges and takes on a systematic form that tends to dominate that society as a structure of verbal authority.

I call this verbal culture that grows up in and tries to control and unify a society, so far as words can do so, a myth of concern. I call it a myth, or more accurately a mythology, because it is usually contained in some kind of narrative (*mythos*) or story framework. It is often called an ideology, but I find that term rather restricting, though I may use it occasionally. And I speak of concern rather than belief, because a general public assent to certain formulas is more important to a society than actual belief in them. Belief may be in theory the essential thing, but private beliefs elude social vigilance, as the public expression of them does not.

Such myths of concern may be centred either in the religious or in the political area, but they always contain an element of both. Myths we call religious, like those of Christianity, Islam, or Buddhism, must operate within some political context; political myths, democratic, Marxist, or fascist, must have a religious dimension as well. In some societies there is one dominating myth of concern, where everyone must express agreement with its main principles, or at least refrain from open disagreement. In others, including our own, there may be subordinate myths of concern, Christian or Marxist or what not, operating as pressure groups.

As a society grows, its central concerns, which are largely undifferentiated at first, begin to develop into the more varied and specific forms of culture and civilization. Literature, music, science, religion become distinguishable and self-contained areas, even though there may be no sharp boundary lines. In proportion as they develop, the inner laws of their own structures become more clearly visible, and the extent to which they are permitted to follow their own line of development determines the level of civilization in society.

The arts and sciences thus have two poles, a social pole of origin in the human sense of concern, where the artist or scientist does something primarily because his society thinks it important for him to do it, and an opposite pole in the structure of the art or science itself, where he follows the inner laws of that structure and finds himself making technical discoveries within it. One pole is that of accountability to society, the other of fidelity to the laws of a discipline of growing autonomy and coherence. The two poles do not, in theory, have to be inconsistent with each other, but in practice there is likely to be a good deal of tension between them.

Science will give us clearer examples than the arts. The science of astronomy, in the time of Galileo, had to break free of the mythological concern for believing in a geocentric universe, and biology and geology, in the time of Darwin, had to break free of the concern for belief in a divine creation taking place six thousand years previously. Apart altogether from the persecution of social dissidents, similar oppositions have arisen between Soviet science and doctrines inferred from the nineteenth-century myth of Marxism. In these examples it is the myth of concern that seems clearly wrong or obsolete, but in such issues as the atom bomb, atmospheric pollution, and energy crisis, social concern clearly has its own case. But because the material benefits of allowing the sciences to develop their own structures are so obvious, there is usually a working agreement in most countries that the sciences ought to keep some autonomy as disciplines as well as remaining accountable to society, and that the scientist may preserve a loyalty to his science as well as to his country. The arts are not so fortunate, and literature is the least fortunate of all.

Extreme proponents of a dominant concern are very unwilling to admit that literature has any authority or even structural basis of its own worth bothering about, and maintain that all literature should say what the dominant myth wants it to say, or at least determine itself by the dialectics of that myth. About two generations ago, there was a sentimental enthusiasm for the Middle Ages as a time when all aspects of culture were united under the banner of a single myth of concern, and Marxism, at least until recently, used a similar sales pitch. Even among broader-minded readers and students of literature we often find a concern that literature should not get too literary, or criticism too free from the clichés of social anxiety. It seems obvious that literature should have some accountability to society, just as science does, otherwise it would have no identifiable social function at all. But the expression of social concern, whatever species of concern may dominate a given society, has too often been hysterical and superstitious, too obviously an issue of maintaining authority without criticism, to be fully trusted. Shakespeare himself had a vigilant and by no means stupid censorship to contend with, and avoided it so expertly that he turned a negative achievement into a positive asset.

Literature develops out of human concern, admittedly, and it is not only legitimate but inevitable that criticism should study works of literature as a reflection or mirror of the social and historical concerns from which they arose. But as soon as we have several works of literature we become aware of the different ways in which they reflect one another, and this becomes intensified when we have many works in a single convention or genre. It is from the study of the conventions and genres that are grouped around such words as 'comedy' that we begin to get a glimpse into the authority of literature, an authority which derives from its integrity as a structure rather than from its fidelity as a mirror of its time. Literature, like science, requires loyalty and commitment from serious writers, even when that loyalty conflicts with social demands.

The traditional way of defending myths of concern consists largely of denouncing all the others, and it is still perhaps broadly true that most myths of concern ultimately want to destroy all other such myths. But when competing myths of concern can bring about such appalling disaster if the social power they represent is stupid or bigoted, it is clearly time to look for common underlying factors as a basis of possible coexistence. The immediate question that this situation leads to seems to be, are there common themes that underlie all possible myths of concern?

For an answer to this we have first to look at society in the limit-situation of crisis. It is when a society is at war, or, far more clearly, when it is faced by a natural crisis like a plague, a famine, a flood, or an earthquake, that it becomes obvious that real human concerns are much fewer and simpler than the complications of religious and political mythologies may suggest. In any case, in such a situation two essential human concerns invariably loom up in the foreground: survival and deliverance.

By deliverance, as something distinct from survival itself, I mean the expansion of consciousness or energy that we often expect or experience or hope for when we pass through a crisis of survival. Those of us who remember living through the Second World War will remember also how often we were told that we had to win the peace as well as the war. The assumption was that a new and greatly expanded life would await us as soon as the war was over. This was an illusion of considerable importance in sustaining democratic morale, and when the war ended it disappeared, having performed its function. But the myth of deliverance is not always a deliberately summoned up mirage of this kind. On the contrary, it seems to be at the core of every major myth of concern.

In Christianity deliverance appears in the conception of salvation; in Buddhism it is the goal of enlightenment; in Judaism it is the restoration of Israel; in Marxism it is equality in a classless society; in democracy it is the attaining of personal and social liberty. In ordinary human history, however, myths of concern are preoccupied with the survival of the institutions in which they are embodied. In order to safeguard these institutions, the actual goal of deliverance becomes something to be indefinitely postponed, associated either with a future from which only posterity will benefit, or with life after death in a 'next' world. But in a developed and pluralistic culture, we said, literature achieves an authority of its own along with a relatively autonomous structure. What does literature, by itself, have to say about survival and deliverance? The question becomes especially significant when the institutions embodying concern lose their perspective on such things.

We notice that some words in religion, such as 'conversion' in Christianity or *paravritti* (turning around) in Buddhism, or 'revolution' in political ideology, emphasize the fact that one thing necessary is a reversing of the normal current of life. Other words, such as 'enlightenment' or 'salvation,' emphasize rather the sense of recognition that accompanies this process. Reversal and recognition, then, seem to be structural principles outside literature, which suggests that a study of them inside literature may provide at least some interesting analogies to social concern from literature, and analogies that have become, as it were, distinct species and not merely derived varieties.

It seems to me that the conventions and genres grouped around the term 'romance' have much to do with the human concern for survival, and that the conventions and genres grouped around the term 'comedy' have much to do with the human concern for deliverance. Romance is a narrative form throwing its main emphasis on linear movement. Its primary appeal is to keep one listening or turning the pages or coming back for a further instalment, as in the old cliffhanger movie serials, or in Scheherezade's strategy to stop her story at a point where her repulsive husband's curiosity to find out what happened next will be stronger than his sadism. In the vast eighteenth-century Chinese romance formerly called in English *The Dream of the Red Chamber*, and now known as *The Story of the Stone*, each chapter ends with the formula: 'if you want to know how this turned out, read the next chapter.' The formula is essentially the same in, say, Ariosto, at the other end of the world's culture. The kernel of romance is a series of adventures, in other words romance is a discontinuous form of narrative in which a hero or heroine or both survive a number of crises. If they survive them in unexpected ways, so much the better for the reader's interest. The most primitive type of romance is an endless form, like contemporary comic strips, and while literal endlessness is not possible for frail human mortality, romances are often extended to enormous length if the sequential formula seems to be working satisfactorily.

In most forms of comedy, on the other hand, at least the New Comedy with which Shakespeare was mainly concerned, the emphasis is on a teleological plot, usually one with a mystery in it which is disclosed in or near a final recognition scene. The emphasis is not on sequence, but on moving toward a climax in which the end incorporates the beginning. The climax is a vision of deliverance or expanded energy and freedom. This may be expressed socially, individually, or in other ways, but however it is expressed, we normally have a vision of a group of people going off the stage or page to begin a new kind of life. As the audience is excluded from this new life, its quality is left undefined: we are, as a rule, simply told that they are going to be happy.

I have explained this more fully elsewhere, and repeat it here only to clarify what follows. The essential drive in comedy is toward liberation, whether of the central character, a pair of lovers, or its whole society, and so comedy has the same narrative shape as many of the programmes in religion that lead toward goals of salvation or enlightenment or beatitude. In Aristotle, where reversal is treated mainly as a structural principle of tragedy, something in an action exceeding the bounds of what is given to the human situation (*hyper moron*, beyond fate, is Homer's phrase for this) is reversed by the returning power of nature or divine will or opposed human force. Such a reversal operates within the general framework of law. But the parallels suggested between comedy and myths of deliverance make us wonder whether the typical comic reversal may not transcend the framework of law altogether, as the work of a redeeming or rescuing force opposed to the normal movement of circumstances.

Some works of literature we instinctively call comedies: with others we may ask: 'is this play really a comedy?' or some similar question. Such questions have meaning and are worth discussing in some connections, but we should be aware that comedy is a context word and not an essence word. If a play in a theatre is subtitled 'a comedy,' information is being conveyed to a potential audience about what kind of thing to expect, and this type of information has been intelligible since before the days of Aristophanes. But to answer the question of whether it really 'is' a comedy or not would involve us in a limiting definition of the essence of comedy, as a something not found in other things, whereas comedy is a term indicating a certain grouping of literary phenomena which may be found to a greater or lesser extent anywhere in literature. There has never been such a 'thing' as comedy, though most people are familiar with the range and ambience of what the word indicates.

In Greek drama the form used by Aristophanes is so different from the form used by Aeschylus that we almost have the illusion of there being such a thing as comedy. Hence Samuel Johnson's remark about Shakespeare's plays, that they are strictly neither tragedies nor comedies, but compositions of a distinct kind. Still, I think everyone experiences tragedy in *King Lear* for all its grotesque comedy, and comedy in *Measure for Measure* for all its painful scenes. Socrates' remark at the end of the *Symposium*, that the same man might be capable of both tragedy and comedy, seems to imply that tragedy and comedy were not, for Plato, forms or ideas, but aspects of them. A critic accustomed to thinking in Platonic terms would perhaps draw the inference that survival and deliverance and other such myths of concern were the real forms, and religious or literary formulations of them only imitations. I should prefer to try to do without the 'real forms,' and leave such words as tragedy and comedy plastic enough to account for their varieties, without getting trapped into thinking in terms of essences or realities in a higher world which poetry reflects. A myth of deliverance, in any case, can be found in either tragedy or comedy, but the shapes given to the expressions of the myth will differ accordingly.

Let us look at the *Odyssey* for an illustration of some of the structural principles of romance and comedy. The *Odyssey* is divided into twenty-four books: whoever made this division or whenever it was made, it is a very accurate analysis of the actual proportions of the poem. The twenty-four books break into two parts of twelve books each. In the first twelve books we have all the characteristics of romance, a sequence of exciting adventures that the hero manages to squirm out of each time. These twelve books are, so to speak, a circumference looking for a centre. Odysseus wants to get home, but, like a baseball player, he has to go around in a circle to get there. At first base there is Calypso, the goddess who wants him to be her husband, and promises him immortality if he will stay with her. At second base there is Circe, who is willing to accept him as a lover in default of being able to turn him into a pig. At third base there is Nausicaa, whom it is proposed he should marry, settling down with her in Phaeacia.

The return of Odysseus is a contrast with three other returns, those of Ajax, Agamemnon, and Menelaus. The return of Ajax is a tragedy caused by the hero's own *hybris*; that of Agamemnon is a tragedy too, but a tragedy of a different type. In Aeschylus it is

primarily a revenge tragedy because Clytemnestra's murder of
Agamemnon when he gets home has, for at least its professed
motive, his earlier sacrifice of their daughter Iphigeneia, and this
outrage in the past is reinforced by one in the present, the bringing
back of Cassandra as a slave-mistress. Menelaus is, Homer says,
by virtue of having married and regained a daughter of Zeus, to be
carried off to Elysium or the Happy Islands at his death. What
shape the return of Odysseus is to be is left in doubt until it is clear
that his desire to return home to Penelope and Ithaca is a steadfast
one.

This suggests that the return of Odysseus seems to be at least
partly dependent on his own courage and persistence, even though
it could not have been accomplished without the help of Athene.
Obvious as this sounds, it is a point that has to be established at the
beginning. The *Odyssey* opens with a speech of Zeus explaining
that gods are not to be blamed for human woes because human
beings bring their woes on themselves. His example is Aesgisthus,
the lover of Clytemnestra, who has been killed by Orestes. Like
other theologians, Zeus chooses his examples rather selectively:
Aesgisthus is a clear instance of villainy meeting its just deserts,
but the more ambiguous and perplexing cases of Agamemnon and
Orestes themselves are passed over. Still, the implication that
human beings play some role in determining the outcome of their
own fortunes enables Athene to make out a case for the safe
return of Odysseus.

The second half of the poem, the last twelve books, is in one
of the typical shapes of comedy rather than of romance. The
setting is Odysseus' house in Ithaca, and throughout these last
twelve books Odysseus has the comic role of the hero who starts
as the character least likely to succeed. He begins as a despised,
unrecognized, and anonymous beggar whose tales about himself
to Eumaeus and others almost raise questions about his actual

identity. Gradually he becomes a stronger and stronger force, is reunited with his son Telemachus, and then with his wife, and finally overthrows the perverted social order represented by the suitors and emerges as master of his house. Various themes from the first or romance half of the poem seem to be repeated in different contexts: there are repetitions of the themes of descent to the lower world, of disguised identity, of marriage, of ordeals that only the hero can pass, and the treacherous companions who steal the oxen of the sun seem a kind of parallel to the suitors. If the romance half of the *Odyssey* is a circumference looking for a centre, the second or comic half is a centre gradually expanding into a circumference.

The *Odyssey*, in its comic half, presents a very different plot, at least superficially, from the typical New Comedy plot of several centuries later. In that plot, a festive society, generally featuring the sexual union of young people, is born out of a perverted or absurd social order, represented mainly by their parents, which is in charge of things at the beginning of the play. Yet the *Odyssey* preserves the essentials of the same kind of thing: the heroine Penelope is delivered from what in other stories would have been a band of robbers or pirates; the perverted order represented by the suitors is destroyed and the proper order restored; there is no antagonism between father and son, but it is the union of the two that makes the *dénouement* possible.

Some features of the second half of the *Odyssey* remind us of similar features in Shakespeare. The main emphasis, as in *The Winter's Tale*, falls on the reconciliation and reunion of an older couple – Homer shows no interest in providing a bride for Telemachus. Then again, Athene's activity on behalf of Odysseus sometimes expands into a kind of stage manager role, disguising Odysseus in the forms most advantageous for him at the moment, and reminding us of the stage management of, say, Prospero in

The Tempest. And while the entire *Odyssey* is dominated by the theme of *nostos* or return, the second half, which never leaves Ithaca, is concentrated on a growing self-actualizing of the hero, like the growth of Prince Hal from prodigal to hero in *Henry IV*.

Both halves of the *Odyssey* are 'literary,' in the sense that the kind of thing that happens is the kind of thing that happens only in stories. But the second half seems to have a closer analogy to the moral and religious standards connected with the heroic ethos of Homer, of a kind that makes it authoritative for its culture as well as simply entertaining. Thus the descent of the suitors to Hades in Book XXIV has an ethical dimension lacking in the more primitive account of the gathering of the souls of the dead in Book XI. In any case it is clear that the climax of the poem, Odysseus' reconquest of his son, wife, and household, is a gigantic reversal of the situation we encounter in the opening book, with the suitors wasting his substance, Telemachus and Penelope impotent to resist them, and the hero himself far away, perhaps dead. Further, the reversal of the situation is not simply that, but a growth in the identity of Odysseus himself, as son, wife, and household become his 'property,' in the Aristotelian sense of what is proper to him and a part of his real self.

The general shape of the *Odyssey* plot, where the hero is banished or exiled, returns in disguise, and finally claims his own, may be found in any number of folktales and literary works. It seems so central to imaginative experience that it would be even surprising if it did not turn up somewhere in Shakespeare. In fact it occurs several times in different forms, but the one most useful for our purposes is the story in *Measure for Measure*, to which we must now turn.

There seems no way out of summarizing the story for expository purposes, however well known it may be. Vincentio, the Duke of Vienna (which Shakespeare seems to have thought of as an Italian town), leaves his deputy Angelo as regent to administer a remarkably unenlightened law providing the death penalty for adultery, but returns disguised as a friar to see what will happen. The young man Claudio, betrothed and legally married to Julietta except for a public announcement of the betrothal, has intercourse with her and is condemned to death.

Claudio's sister Isabella, the heroine, is physically and intellectually mature, and not only mature but unusually attractive and intelligent. Her emotional development, however, has lagged behind, and her intense desire to become a nun seems to be prompted more by an adolescent girl's fear of the world than by a genuine vocation. We suspect this at her first appearance where, though not yet even a novice, she tells a senior nun with great confidence that she would prefer 'a more strict restraint' in the convent. There is also a strong father-fixation that comes out in a later speech. Poets are often supposed not to have known about such things before Freud 'discovered' them, but Shakespeare, inspecting the sexual mores of Vienna centuries earlier, obviously saw much the same phenomena.

When Lucio, a young man about town, comes to tell Isabella that her brother has beeen condemned to death, she is still lost in her dream of a recluse life, and reacts as though she were half asleep. Under Lucio's prodding she finally goes to plead with Angelo for her brother's life, and under further prodding begins really to enter the role. Very soon she finds that she can save Claudio at the price of being seduced by Angelo. She visits Claudio in the prison and tells him this, and Claudio, with the horror of an imminent death fresh on him, urges her to save him by yielding to Angelo. Isabella explodes in a furious tirade, and the action appears to end in a deadlock.

The 'legal' situation involved is one that can be explained from a study of the social and historical background of Shakespeare's

day. Most modern audiences would probably find the law the disguised Duke is so anxious to have enforced a sick and silly law,
but Shakespeare, with his infallible instinct for keeping out of
trouble, never says so, or in fact says anything at all that could
possibly be construed as an attack on the anxieties of his contemporaries. The play is speaking to us with the independent authority of drama itself, and to understand it we must ignore the gabble
of rationalizations that many of Shakespeare's contemporaries
would automatically have started going in their minds, and listen
to what the play is telling us by its action. The framework of
Isabella's speech is, of course, nominally Christian. Its giveaway is
in the line 'I'll pray a thousand prayers for thy death.' Nobody in
the remotest shape of a Christian could start offering prayers for a
brother's death: a recluse nun who did that would have mistaken
her calling. A real saint, whatever her course of action, would
have shown some sympathy with and compassion for Claudio's
plight – in short, if we were to take such a line seriously we should
have to regard Isabella as a somewhat sinister character.

But, of course, we cannot take it seriously. There is nothing
fundamentally wrong with Isabella, as the disguised Duke well
realizes, but she is totally demoralized. She has had her first direct
glimpse of the evil in human nature that she has previously only
read or heard about in books and sermons. Perhaps we are also
intended to suspect that something in her has been more attracted
both by Angelo and by his proposition than she would ever have
dreamed possible, and that a suppressed recognition of this is at the
heart of her misery. It is even possible that the gradual warming of
her interest in pleading for Claudio's life had more to do with
Angelo than with Claudio. In any case the action of the play,
which has been uniformly sombre and menacing up to this point,
appears to be heading for unrelieved tragedy. Claudio is about to
die for an act that most of the characters who comment on it

clearly regard as trifling; Angelo has been revealed to the audience as the most contemptible kind of hypocrite, the kind who tries to make himself feel better by despising himself. Isabella might, in theory, return to the convent, but her dream of a sheltered life devoted to prayer and contemplation has been shattered for ever.

The Duke himself seems to be merely dodging his responsibilities: his apparent confidence that his precious law will work if it is only enforced is ironically illustrated by the fact that it gets a firm grip on Claudio, who is a decent person, but fumbles badly with the actual pimps. He makes an eloquent speech attempting to reconcile Claudio to his fate, but, apart from the fact that the speech is not a Christian speech but a purely Stoic one, it completely fails of its ostensible purpose. In that context he has no more power of redemption than anyone else. The only person in the first half of the play who seems to do anything sensible is Lucio, but Lucio has no real generosity: he will try to help Claudio because he regards Claudio as a gentleman, but refuses to bail the pimp Pompey because he is not. As in most tragic actions, the characters in it have no knowledge of themselves. Angelo, for example, in attempting, or rather pretending, to struggle with his temptation, says of the devil:

> O cunning enemy, that to catch a saint,
> With saints dost bait thy hook!

He calls Isabella a saint, which is intelligible in this context, but he also calls himself a saint, which indicates that he still has a lot to learn about himself, and through himself about human nature.

At a very clearly marked point in the prison scene, Act III, scene i, line 150, the disguised Duke steps forward to speak to Isabella, and the rhythm switches abruptly from blank verse to prose. This is the first sign that we are in an entirely new ball game: the play breaks in two as sharply as a diptych. From here on we are engaged in a comic action, an extremely complicated intrigue involving a bed trick, endless disguisings, and many lies. The action is stage-managed by the disguised Duke, who takes on a role that is frequent and very important in Shakespeare, of a kind of deputy dramatist, arranging a dramatic action within the larger design.

The clearest example of such a deputy dramatist role in Shakespeare is that of Prospero in *The Tempest*, who sets up the whole action of the play, so to speak, within the play. Hamlet, too, is responsible not only for an actual play within the play, but creates a great variety of sub-dramatic roles, lunatic, lover, poet, intriguer, avenger, soliloquizer, and others, enacted by himself. Such deputy dramatist figures in Shakespeare usually have very long and elaborate speaking parts. In *Othello*, for instance, Iago's speaking role is longer than Othello's own, because Iago is the demonic producer of the terrible foreground action. Similarly, Duke Vincentio in *Measure for Measure* has the longest speaking role of any character in Shakespeare's comedies, and he shows a producer's concern for timing, the extending of suspense to the limit, the positioning of the characters in the right lighting, and so on.

We get some curious modifications of this role in Shakespeare. *King Lear*, we said, begins with Lear's ambitious but inept design of staging a big dramatic scene of love and loyalty around himself. In the deposition scene in *Richard II*, Richard is losing his crown to Bolingbroke while stage-managing a dramatic performance in which Bolingbroke has a secondary part. The stage-managing of her own death scene by Cleopatra needs no elaboration. A similar though minor form of the device is, I think, involved in the use of Lucio in *Measure for Measure* itself.

In each of the three problem comedies there is a character, Lucio, Parolles, Thersites, who is a compulsive talker, unable to stop even when he is clearly getting into trouble, and much given to slander. We shall try to account for the significance of such a character, who represents the irresponsible use of words, later on. But in *Measure for Measure* Lucio is also a kind of counter-producer, with his own show to put on. He has no end in view beyond wanting to keep the brothels open, and is not a serious competitor of the Duke, but he acts as a kind of lightning-rod in the play: that is, he prevents us from taking the Duke completely at his own valuation. For the most part we are asked to accept folktale conventions in the plot, where a ruler, like Haroun al Raschid, moves disguised through his people, and in which a pious friar talks a pious young woman into a very dubious scheme designed to immobilize her seducer. Our realistic responses are in abeyance, but they are still operating: we do not wholly lose sight of the fact that in real life the Duke would be an intolerable snoop. Lucio's reckless slanders to the disguised Duke about himself remind us that in real life listeners seldom hear much good of themselves, and even more seldom deserve to. Similarly, in the final scene Lucio keeps getting laughs as the Duke blusters at him, keeping the scene in just enough balance to prevent it from dissolving into melodrama.

Measure for Measure, then, is a dramatic diptych of which the first part is a tragic and ironic action apparently heading for unmitigated disaster, and the second part an elaborate comic intrigue which ends by avoiding all the disasters. The next question clearly is: what is the significance of such a construction, and what light does the structure throw on the play's meaning? All the answers to this have to begin with the fact that *Measure for Measure* is not a play about the philosophy of government, the responsibilities of rulers, the social problem of prostitution, or any of the things that so many commentators insist that it is. It is a play about the relation of all such things to the structure of comedy. And because comedy is a context word and not an essence word, the phrase 'structure of comedy' means among other things the reflection of other comedies in *Measure for Measure*.

Measure for Measure, then, is a comedy about comedy, as *Hamlet* is a tragedy about tragedy, and as the history plays are plays about history (more particularly history as seen through the actions of royalty) considered as a theatrical performance. We notice that many plays of the time begin with prologues indicating the role that theatrical convention is about to play in what follows. *Mucedorus*, for instance, begins with a dialogue between 'Envy' and 'Comedy' in which Envy prophesies many threatening complications in the action, but Comedy assures the audience that everything will ultimately turn out well. An old play called *The Rare Triumphs of Love and Fortune* begins with a similar debate between Fortuna and Venus. I mention these two examples of a very common convention (we could go as far afield as the opening of Monteverdi's *Coronation of Poppaea*) for two reasons. First, they are both plays that Shakespeare seems to have been reading or re-reading about the time he was writing his final romances (or seeing: *Mucedorus* was having a revival). Second, they are both rather simple-minded plays of the public theatre, and remind us that what may seem at first sight a sophisticated convention, of introducing personifications of the actual structure of the play itself, is in fact a feature of popular drama, to which Shakespeare's loyalties were very deep.

We began by saying that a work of literature has two poles, its origin in the conditions of its time and its place in the structure of literature itself. As a reflection of its own time, a play may reflect many things, including the general framework of assumptions and values and moral standards that Shakespeare's audience could be assumed to have brought into the theatre with them. This framework at the time would have had a general Christian shape, and it has often been noticed that *Measure for Measure* (though the phrase itself is used by Shakespeare in other contexts) takes its title from the New Testament, and seems to be concerned with some version of the Christian contrast between law and grace, in which the former is found to be insufficient without the latter. If we attend only to the contemporary reference of the play, we may feel that it looks like a Christian allegory, with political overtones. But, first, our experience of the play tells us that it is not an allegory, and, second, no contemporary of Shakespeare who wanted to see a Christian allegory on the stage would be very well satisfied with *Measure for Measure*.

The Merchant of Venice also deals with the superseding of the law by grace, of justice by mercy, of trusting to a bond by forgiveness. It is hardly a Christian allegory either, but it is a step closer to being one, because its central blocking character is explicitly identified as a Jew, who is contrasted with a spirit referred to as 'Christian,' and alleged to be full of charity and good will. Because of these identifications, it is also a step closer to melodrama, as melodrama is more of a direct reflection of the audience's pre-established moral values. We may feel that the Shylock-Jew identification, in particular, blurs the immediacy of the play for us and makes it more of a historical document, though of course this does not affect the skill of the dramaturgy. From our present point of view, *Measure for Measure*, which deals with legalism and forgiveness simply as aspects of human life, expresses the authority of comedy much more unequivocally than *The Merchant of Venice*, being less dependent on references to what is established outside comedy.

According to ancient critics working on an Aristotelian basis, the action of comedy is assisted by the machinery of certain devices, classified as oaths, compacts, laws, witnesses, and ordeals. All five of these are heavily featured in the action of *Measure for Measure*, but the one that concerns us at the moment is the ordeal. Three major male characters, Claudio, Angelo, and Lucio, are all brought face to face with death: the Duke himself, in disguise, is threatened with the rack, and the Provost with disgrace and dismissal. The Greek word for ordeal (basanos) also means touchstone, and facing death is an ordeal designed in part to reveal one's genuine character. Claudio is under sentence of death during nearly all the play: this belongs to a common structural principle of comedy, which is part of its function in presenting a theatrical form of deliverance. It is found in the otherwise very light-hearted Comedy of Errors. Claudio is capable of courage and resignation, but he is no masochist, and is young enough, and feels innocent enough, to want desperately to live. Angelo has been conditioned to feel that death is the lawful penalty for certain acts, and in a state of despair he is ready to welcome the application of that principle to himself. Lucio ignores the threats of whipping and hanging, and protests only against the violation of his comfortable double standard of sexuality, in being forced to marry the woman who has borne him a child.

Yet nobody comes out of the play much damaged: Shakespeare seems to go out of his way to emphasize this point. An imprisoned pirate expires of natural causes, but even the condemned murderer Barnardine, who has previously refused to be beheaded on the ground that it will not cure his headache, gets away with his refusal and is finally allowed to go free. Instead of all these deaths, three suspended marriages are completed, and a fourth between the Duke and Isabella seems indicated at the end. We begin to wonder if the bed trick, the device which both condemns Angelo and saves his life, and is the central image of the play, does not represent a rite of passage from death to new life. We notice that a beautiful image of Claudio, uttered during the prison scene, is among other things a grotesque anticipation of the bed trick image:

> If I must die,
> I will encounter darkness as a bride,
> And hug it in mine arms!

In any case the title of the play seems to imply some analogy between the action of the comedy and the struggle of legalism and forgiveness in Christianity, though, as we said, not the kind of dependent analogy that would make the play allegorical. In the first half of the play, Claudio is betrothed to Julietta and anticipates his marital rights before making a public announcement; Angelo is engaged to Mariana and breaks off the engagement because the financial arrangements fall through. Legally, this makes Claudio a condemned criminal and Angelo a model of virtue; but there can hardly be an audience in the world that could not see what nonsense this legal valuation is. As we saw earlier, in glancing at the farcical scene with Pompey and Elbow, the law as such is often incompetent even to identify the right people as lawbreakers, much less improve the quality of life. In short, the situation in the first half of the play is founded on what Christianity calls the knowledge of good and evil, the perspective of trial and judgment, with accusers and defenders, that runs all through its central mythology. The knowledge of good and evil was forbidden to Adam and Eve, and from this play we can, within the context of comedy, see why: it is not a genuine knowledge of anything, including good and evil.

Of the three threatened characters, Angelo cannot escape from the legalistic perspective by himself, but is pulled out of it by the fact that he is genuinely loved by Mariana. His relation to her is a miniature version of Bertram's relation to Helena in *All's Well*, of which more later. Lucio alone remains untouched by the action, as he has nothing of the power of self-analysis that his opposite number in *All's Well*, Parolles, does have. Lucio is completely a product of a society dominated by the knowledge of good and evil, which, we said, is not a real knowledge even of that. When he calls Isabella 'a thing enskyed and sainted,' this is clearly a tribute to her, but it is also an expression of his own immaturity about women, which finds nuns and whores easier to understand than the vast majority of women who are neither, because nuns and whores can be clearly labelled 'good' and 'bad.' But adopting such labels does not go with knowledge, only with reflecting conventions. Lucio has no awareness whatever of being good or bad, merely of doing or not doing what is accepted in his circle. He utters slanders because he speaks according to 'the trick,' the fashion, and fornicates because that is done too.

However, all these disclosures of character are subordinate to the speech Isabella gives in response to Mariana's appeal, urging the forgiveness of Angelo. At the time of making the speech, she knows that Angelo has tried to make her the instrument of a peculiarly loathsome hypocrisy, and she also thinks he has double-crossed her and sentenced Claudio to be executed after all. Nevertheless, the woman who earlier had stated her intention of praying for Claudio's death pleads for Angelo's life on the ground that he is less villainous than self-deluded.

As soon as she makes this speech we understand that this is really what the whole second half of the play has been about. The primary end and aim of everything the Duke is doing is to get that speech out of her, and the state of morality in Vienna could not matter less. Far less of a rhetorical set speech than Portia's speech on mercy, it expresses the genuine kind of love, the charity which is the supreme virtue, that Isabella had dimly in mind when she first wanted to be a nun. Isabella herself, perhaps, could not always live on the level of nobility that that speech represents, but there has been a moment in which her essential self spoke; and such moments may become foci around which all the rest of one's life may revolve. Passion and accusation (parodied in the fornication and slander of Lucio) are reversed into the fusion of love and wisdom that makes humanity redeemable.

We noticed that in the structure of tragedy there is a reversing movement known as *nemesis*, the dialectic counter-movement to the aggressiveness of the hero. If *Measure for Measure* possessed a character on a genuinely heroic scale, this *nemesis*-reversal would be the kind we should expect from the action of the first half of the play. The phrasing in the New Testament passage which the title of the play echoes, 'and with what measure ye mete, it shall be measured to you again,' points to this kind of tragic reversal. But the reversal in *Measure for Measure*, carried out by the Duke but dependent also on the genuine sanctity of Isabella, is full of improbability and absurdity, yet none the less it triumphs over the armoured tanks of self-righteousness so completely that we are no longer in this measuring world when the play ends. The law has been, not annulled or contradicted, but transcended; not broken but fulfilled by being internalized.

One feature of the play that seems puzzling at first is the emphatic assertion that the effectiveness of law depends on the personal integrity of the lawgiver. This is not true of ordinary experience: all Shakespeare's historical plays, for example, make the point that the effectiveness of the ruler depends on his will, not on his morality. The point *Measure for Measure* makes is rather different. Society depends on law, but law at its best can only define the law-breaker: from the point of view of the law, an honest man is one who has never been convicted of stealing. But society could hardly hold together with a standard as low as that: morality must rise at least to morale before it can function at all. What holds society together are the honest men, the individuals who impose a much more rigorous standard of honesty on themselves.

But to try to embody individual discipline in social legislation would result in the most frightful tyranny: society as such must be left more flexible. If Angelo were the model of disciplined rectitude that he is assumed to be at first, his enforcing of the law would be theoretically justifiable, but such enforcing is really a projection of his own self-conflicts, and sooner or later he, or anyone else in his position, will collapse under the strain. That is why the Duke himself cannot stay and administer his own law: if he did it would break him and there would be no redeeming force left in the action. So while the law is transcended by the Duke's general forgiveness, it is fulfilled at the same time: what he does is to break down the antithesis between individual and social reformation. It works with everyone except Lucio, and Lucio's anonymous wife may yet do something even for him.

We may note at this point that the same diptych construction, the same halfway break, occurs later in *The Winter's Tale*, in the transition between winter in Sicilia and spring in Bohemia. An action proceeding towards unrelieved gloom and disaster ends with Antigonus leaving the infant Perdita in Bohemia and being pursued by a bear. Again, in a precisely marked spot, Act III, scene iii, line 57, the rhythm switches suddenly from blank verse to prose with the entry of the two Bohemian shepherds, and a different action begins. (The break does *not* occur quite where we should expect it, at the beginning of Act IV with Time introduced as a chorus to tell us that sixteen years have gone by.) Shakespeare practically abandons Greene's *Pandosto*, the story he has been retelling up to that point, and a highly complicated comic structure with two recognition scenes in it follows. The difference from *Measure for Measure* is that there seems to be no deputy dramatic figure for the second action, unless Apollo, working through Paulina and an offstage oracle, has theatrical ambitions, as Jupiter appears to have in *Cymbeline* and Diana in *Pericles*. In *The*

Tempest the deputy dramatist figure reappears in Prospero, but this play, which is an unusually short one, is concerned only with the second half of the diptych action. The first part has taken place before the play begins, and its last episode, the wrecking of Alonso's ship, is the first scene of the play we have.

These parallels with two of the romances merely establish that the reversal of action in *Measure for Measure* is not an accident or a stunt, but something deeply involved with Shakespeare's romantic conception of comedy. The 'problem' comedies anticipate the romances more clearly than Shakespeare's other earlier comedies, and *Measure for Measure*, in particular, anticipates them in the way that it contains, instead of simply avoiding, a tragic action. What we are seeing is a myth of deliverance, with some resemblances to the myths of deliverance we already know, more particularly the Christian ones familiar to Shakespeare's audience, although *The Winter's Tale* has a strong admixture of Classical myth as well, such as the Demeter-Proserpine story. But resemblances are structural analogies only, not keys to interpretation. I cannot imagine Shakespeare speaking of the theatre, as Bernard Shaw does, as 'that older and greater church to which I belong' – that kind of self-consciousness does not seem to be in his makeup. But none the less he writes as though he knew that the theatre was a great and catholic institution with its own traditions, its own conventions, and its own authority.

We normally identify verbal authority with the language of doctrines and concepts and ideas. This would be the authority for the 'problem' plays too if they really were problem plays in the sense of being media for issues or observations outside the conventions of comedy. The purpose of the reversal of action we have dealt with in *Measure for Measure* is to prevent it from becoming a problem play in the ordinary sense. The reversal forces it solidly and securely into the mould of comic convention. Nothing extra-dramatic to which the play points is outside it; whatever is not in the play, or is there in addition to the play, is in front of it, in the shared experience of the audience. In other societies, or in this one, man may learn about freedom and deliverance also from his religion, from his political ideology, from various wise men or gurus, even from exploring his own consciousness. One's view of such things will be incomplete until we have paid some attention also to the high mysteries of comedy that Shakespeare has in his keeping, and reveals to those who are willing to follow three simple rules: listen to the story; look at the action; and don't think, at least until you know what you're thinking about.

What a man essentially is (and a woman: the usual difficulty with pronouns) is revealed in two ways: by the record of what he has done, and by what he is trying to make of himself, at any given moment. The former is the case of the accuser and relates to the past: it shapes the general form of the tragedy, as we see so powerfully in the conclusion of *Oedipus Rex*. The latter relates to the future, is based on forgiveness and release, and shapes the general form of comedy. The 'problem comedies' give a good deal of attention to both, and so do the romances. All four romances feature a gap of sixteen years or so (before the play begins in *Cymbeline* and *The Tempest*), establishing a pattern of an older and a younger generation, the younger one concerned primarily with its own future, the older one with healing various traumas in its past. A study of the comedy which is in many respects complementary to *Measure for Measure*, *All's Well that Ends Well*, should help to bring this situation into clearer focus.

2

The Reversal of Energy

IN THE PREVIOUS CHAPTER we discussed Aristotle's conception of reversal as a structural principle of drama. Aristotle was mainly concerned with tragedy, and reversal is the structural feature resulting from the fact that the outcome of tragedy is usually the opposite of what the tragic hero hoped for or aimed at. The basis of tragic reversal in Greek drama is normally a process in which a contract of order and balance, supported by gods, human society, and nature itself, recovers its balance after an aggressive act. The recovering of balance is the basis of what is generally called *nemesis*; but the agent of *nemesis*, whether an angry god or a human avenger, is merely the antithesis of the aggressive action. Only if the reversal is accompanied by some form of recognition is there a sense of an action being fulfilled and completed instead of merely neutralized. Such recognition, whatever form it takes, has something in it of an increase of awareness, a move from ignorance to knowledge. Even the most appalling forms of such knowledge, such as Oedipus' knowledge of his relations with his parents or Macbeth's realization that the prophecies given him were only bad jokes, are still knowledge.

This sense of a movement toward knowledge, however, may enlighten the audience as well as the dramatic characters. In Greek tragedy, if the play seems to end with some kind of simplistic pessimism or sense of external fatality, we often find that it is the first play of a trilogy, or otherwise separated from its real context. As the *Oresteia* of Aeschylus proceeds from the murder of Agamemnon to the revenge of Orestes, a chain reaction of neutralized or avenged aggression is set up, which continues a movement started in the house of Argos long before the trilogy of Aeschylus begins. In the last play of the trilogy, *The Eumenides*, this almost mechanical neutralizing force is represented by the Furies, the spirits of vengeance. The Furies, however, have to take a subordinate place in a structure of law which is set up by Athene on the Areopagus. They are thereby transformed into the genuine Eumenides or 'kindly ones,' in a social order of a higher kind, though no less just.

The serene conclusion of *The Eumenides* does not turn the tragic action comic: it completes and fulfils the tragic vision by keeping it within the framework of law. The *Oresteia* trilogy is a tragedy pursued to its final cadence. Terrible things have happened, but we finally get a glimpse of something that makes such things at least assume a shape. This does not mean that we have to accept some moralizing formula of the 'all is best, though we oft doubt' type, but that there is a kind of uncompromising sense in the balancing of *hybris* and *nemesis*, aggression and retribution. If there were no such sense the action could hardly be presented within a dramatic structure at all. The three plays were originally followed by a satyr-play, but the satyr-play seems, using metaphors again, to be related to the previous action spatially rather than consecutively, a contrast of mood rather than a continuing modulation of the action. A parallel example would be the *kyogen* farce that follows the No play in Japanese drama, to which it is still thematically related. Such scenes in Shakespeare as the grave-diggers in *Hamlet*, the porter in *Macbeth*, the Tom o'Bedlam scene in *Lear*, are also not 'comic relief' but spatial expansions of the tragic world, where something grotesque and macabre suddenly thrusts itself up into the rhetoric of heroism.

The Areopagus decision in *The Eumenides*, in which Orestes is acquitted, internalizes the form of law and justice, of which the Furies embody the externalized form. This process of internalizing is an ambiguity involved in most of the Greek words translated roughly as 'fate' (*heimarmene* and others), which may refer either to an arbitrary progression of external events we cannot control, or to a vision of immutable order which is the expanded understanding of the same thing, and which is an expression of a sense of freedom within law rather than of bondage under it. Similarly, justice is the external antagonist of the criminal, but the inner condition of the just man. A parallel expansion and internalizing of such 'fate' encounters us in *Oedipus at Colonus*, where we see, not a comic action, but an enlarged and more comprehensive vision of the Oedipus tragedy.

In comedy, on the other hand, there appear to be two levels of the action: the comic conclusion frequently evades or overrides a law which is often presented as absurd or irrational. A simple example is the humour comedy, of the kind we have in Jonson and Molière, where a central character imposes a foolish law or whim on himself, hypochondria, miserliness, or what not, tries to impose the consequences of this state of mind on others, generally his children, and finds the action of the comedy finally baffling him. In *Measure for Measure*, the law that condemns Claudio can hardly be called whimsical or arbitrary, nor is anything said directly against it: we merely see that the action of the comedy annihilates its social effects. A second look at the play suggests that it is the spirit of legalism itself that is being transcended, rather than any particular law. So while the law is being internalized also in *Measure for Measure*, the leap from crime to forgiveness, from condemnation to redemption, suggests the two levels of action, the movement outside the framework of law altogether, that is typical of comedy, however serious a comedy it may be. *Measure for Measure* is among other things a subtle and searching comedy of humours in which Angelo and Isabella are released from the humours of different kinds of legalism, or what Blake would call moral virtue.

At this point the metaphor of 'structure' is beginning to fail us. The metaphor is drawn from architecture, and suggests something more static than poetry is. In a critical response to any work of literature, we first follow the narrative, in reading or in the theatre, and afterwards we react to it as a totality, with all its parts existing simultaneously. The sense of 'structure,' therefore, originates in the audience after the play ends. But while watching such a play as *Measure for Measure*, what we are aware of at the time is a powerful force encountering still more powerful counter-forces: it is the swirling and contending energies within the play that hold our attention while it is going on. These energies come from the creative energy of the poet, as transmitted to us through the acting of the play. To take our next step we must turn our attention from structure to movement, which involves among other things invoking Plato rather than Aristotle.

Aristotle is interested in poetry; Plato in the poet. Plato's views on the relation of structure to representation are crude compared to Aristotle's; Aristotle's view of the poet as a kind of imitative supermonkey is crude compared to Plato's. Each, when standing on his own ground, sees further and more clearly than any critic has seen since. It is from Aristotle that we get the explanation of the great audience reactions, catharsis and the like, that give literature its permanent social function. It is from Plato that we get the conception of Eros, the heightened energy, with its roots in love, that marks the creative genius.

The dialogue of the *Phaedrus* begins with Socrates commenting on a speech by the rhetorician Lysias which appears to recommend emotional control and more disinterested attitudes in love. Socrates realizes that Eros is an energy so powerful that there can be no question of simply controlling it: it must be turned in a certain direction. Normally, the energy of Eros travels in the direction of Thanatos or death, and the greater the erotic energy, the sooner it gets there. But if the force of love is reversed and sublimated, it becomes a creative force. This reversal is symbolized among other things by the 'palinode' that the poet Stesichorus wrote on the divine beauty of Helen after the gods had struck him blind for writing about her sexual passion.

This leads to the conception of the human psyche as a chariot with two horses, one the noble horse of spiritual love and the other the bucking and plunging horse of passion. If we follow the upward course of sublimated love, it leads us to union with love's objective counterpart, beauty. The vision of love and beauty, in its turn, restores to us the memory of our original state which birth in this world has so largely obliterated. This regained totality of vision is so different from ordinary experience as to seem to the latter a form of madness. And as the conception of love in Socrates is always close to education, the *Phaedrus* is also concerned with the relation between love and genuine eloquence, the right ordering of words. An analogy is involved between the contrast of genuine and wasteful love, and the contrast of genuine creative skill with words and the meretricious skill that produces rhetoric with its appeal to the passions, and sophistry with its appeal to prejudice. This meretricious skill includes the whole approach to poetry that Plato condemns as imitative, using poetry as a self-contained craft rather than as a direct expression of spiritual vision. It is suggested toward the end that even the invention of writing may have a tendency to encourage the self-contained approach. The previous essay should have made it clear that the present book has no interest in following Plato into his rejection of the authority of art.

Some of these conceptions reappear in a very different context in Christianity, where God's love for man (*agape* or *caritas*) is inseparable from the wisdom or Word of God, and is the source of the kind of love that man is intended to develop in response, first back toward God, and secondly toward his neighbour. The New Testament does not use the word *eros*, and classifies the kind of love that is rooted in the sexual instinct as *philia*, which makes it really a form of gregariousness. Hence the reversal and sublimation of love is central in Christianity too, and is connected with its strong emphasis on chastity and celibacy. In the Middle Ages, however, a cult of Eros again developed, owing less to Plato than to Virgil and Ovid. Its focus was heterosexual rather than homosexual, and was based on a close imitation of Christian conceptions, with *eros* replacing *agape*. The underlying assumption of the cult was apparently that the Christian teachings had left something out that was central to human experience and essential to it, especially in poetry.

There is no need to rehearse the familiar story of the growth of the convention of Courtly Love in southern France and its subsequent spread over Europe. We need only remember that love, in the form of unshakable devotion to a mistress, releases a creative power which inspires the hero to great deeds and the poet to great words. This is still the assumed convention in most of Shakespeare. In the sonnets we see the reflection of the view that love is, so to speak, the petrol that runs the poet's engine: a poet who attempts to write without the stimulus of love is assumed conventionally to be a rather poor creature. Devotion to a mistress is still the conventional motivation of the hero in *Troilus and Cressida*, where Hector issues a challenge to the Greek warriors on the basis of the superiority of his lady-love to theirs, though nobody in either the Greek or the Trojan army imagines that Hector's wife Andromache or any other female has anything to do with the challenge.

There are various levels of this Eros cult. In its stricter forms, it was, as in Plato, a sublimated reversal of the normal current of love, a 'vita nuova' or different dimension of experience altogether. Dante's love for Beatrice started at the age of nine and was not diminished by Beatrice's death, but it was not a sexual love and did not affect his marriage, any more than Socrates' homosexual interests affected his marriage to Xanthippe. The theme of reversal in this context appears at the very beginning of the *Inferno*, where Dante encounters three beasts he cannot overcome, but must turn in the opposite direction and be propelled through hell, purgatory, and heaven by the power of love. Dante's love for Beatrice is technically an Eros love, Eros being the god who appears in the *Vita Nuova*; but Beatrice's love for Dante, which makes her an agent of revelation guiding the poet through the heavens of the *Paradiso*, is pure *caritas*.

But while some forms of Courtly Love were highly sublimated, others were not, as we can see if we turn from Dante or Petrarch to *The Romaunt of the Rose* or the story of Tristan and Iseult. By Shakespeare's day love is normally, in comedy, a heterosexual attachment leading to marriage. The tragic form of such love is the *Liebestod*, as we have it in *Romeo and Juliet*, where the heightened energy of love, which transforms Juliet into the most articulate thirteen-year-old in history, meets with an equally heightened catastrophe. We can see in this play how the medieval Courtly Love conventions are still operating as a parallel to Christian doctrines. Strictly speaking, from a Christian point of view, Romeo's suicide might involve him in damnation, but not many in the audience would want to speak as strictly as that. The audience would recognize that Romeo has his own religion: it does not conflict with Christianity or prevent him from going to Friar Laurence for confession, but when he says 'My bosom's lord sits lightly in his throne,' he is speaking of the god to whom he really is committed and who really does run his life, who is Eros. Romeo and Juliet die as saints and martyrs in this god's calendar, just as the 'good women' of Chaucer's *Legend of Good Women* include Dido and Cleopatra, who were also erotic saints and martyrs.

We may add for completeness that Eros is the heightened form of the energy of life itself, which, in a person not capable of love or passion or heroism, is only a mechanical energy that keeps on going until it is exhausted. In some very ironic plays, such as *The Cherry Orchard*, we are shown this life-energy as a repeating habit that, like a wound clock, ticks away until it stops. The central characters in Chekhov's play are presented with various crises and challenges, but they never rise to them, and so their survival is a mere waiting for enough frustration to pile up to end the process. Similarly in many plays of Beckett, where such survival may be symbolized by mutilation, imprisonment, or the paralysis of will. This mere survival, whatever else it may be, is clearly not heroic. In heroic codes survival is a very tepid virtue unless it is continually risked, unless mortal combat or perilous adventure are deliberately sought out. Survival is honourable only when it emerges out of a chance of losing it. When Shakespeare's Cressida deserts Troilus for a Greek lover, she is being very sensible in a way: the fate of captive women in a conquered city will not be hers. But few audiences would find her slithery survival tactics as appealing as the desperate fidelity of Juliet.

We said that it was largely from Virgil and Ovid that medieval and Renaissance poets derived their sense of love as either a destructive passion leading to death or a power that, when reversed or sublimated, may become a transcending of ordinary experience. If we compare Virgil's *Aeneid* with the *Odyssey*, we notice that the *Aeneid*, like its predecessor to which it owes so much, is divided exactly in two, the first six books being a contrast to the next six. The first six, like the first twelve of the *Odyssey*, recount a series of adventures in which a group of refugee Trojans try to reach 'home,' home being in this case not the old Troy but the new one in Italy, though the Homeric theme of *nostos* or return is included in the entire historical cycle of which the poem forms part, because the Dardanians, as the Trojans are also called, came from Italy in the first place. Like Odysseus, Aeneas is decoyed by at least two false homes, Crete and Carthage, before he finally reaches the right one. In the second half of the poem the counterpart to Odysseus' growing mastery of his own house is Aeneas' struggle to establish a bridge-head in Latium, make a dynastic marriage, and undertake various wars and alliances that point in the direction of the founding of Rome.

One hardly expects a strong sexual theme in the story of so *'pius'* a hero, but after all his mother is Venus, who collaborates with Aeneas' enemy Juno to cause Dido of Carthage to fall in love with him. The result is, as far as Dido is concerned, a *Liebestod*, one of the world's great love tragedies. Aeneas deserts her, but he also has to descend to the world of the dead, and when he meets Dido there in Book VI he gets a very humiliating snub. The snub, however, is part of a crucial theme of reversal that begins at that point. Aeneas is told, in a passage which is not only the most frequently quoted passage in the poem but one of the most familiar in all literature, that to descend to the world of the dead is easy enough: it is reversing the movement and going back up again that is difficult:

> facilis descensus Averno;
> noctes atque dies patet atri ianua Ditis;
> sed revocare gradum superasque evadere ad auras,
> hoc opus, hic labor est.

At the end of Book VI, not only does Aeneas himself get back, but we have before that a vision of a number of souls who are to emerge from the shades in the future, as in the Christian myth of the harrowing of hell, as a new dispensation begins for mankind.

The second half of the *Aeneid* contains many of the conventional features associated with comedy, such as love leading to a stable marriage, and the compacts, witnesses, ordeals, and the baffling of the blocking characters that we so often find in comic actions. Juno's opposition continues, but she changes the direction of her strategy, announcing, in a line in Book VII that caught the eye of Freud (who uses it as the motto of his *Traumdeutung*), that if she cannot prevail on the heavens she will stir things up from below:

> flectere si nequeo superos, Acheronta movebo.

One of her most effective allies is Fama or rumour, who, along with slander, has been all through literature an example of the irresponsible and socially disintegrating use of words, the exact opposite of the union of love and true eloquence that is the ideal of the *Phaedrus*.

Aeneas struggles through all his obstacles, but the conclusion of the *Aeneid* is not comic, in the way that the second half of the *Odyssey* is comic, because the real hero of the epic is not Aeneas but Rome, and because everything is pointing forward to the establishing of law, order, the *pax Romana*, and the rule of Caesar many centuries later. The *Aeneid* has rather the feeling of the

Oresteia about it, of tragic struggle forming a final contract to which the divine, human, and natural orders are all parties. The foreground action, ending as it does with the killing of Turnus by Aeneas, suggests that the last part, the part corresponding to *The Eumenides*, dealing with the setting up of law and its social powers, is not being written but is left as a prophecy for Roman readers to supply for themselves. The essential point for us here is that Aeneas is beginning something new in the historical process by turning back the Eros-Thanatos current of passion, adventure, and violent death represented by Dido, making his way up again from the world of the dead that awaits all action as such, and laying the foundation for the great city that rules the world by law. In the sunlight of the Roman *imperium* the gods fade away into ghosts. Juno's opposition seems increasingly to be merely childish, and even Venus is at best only decorative.

The kind of love that triumphs in *Measure for Measure* is again sexual love leading to marriage, and apparently this is to be the direction of Isabella's life as well. The play seems to be a kind of analogue to the Christian principle that charity is the fulfilling of the law, and Isabella's great speech of forgiveness reaches the level of *caritas* without necessarily breaking away from *eros*. The atmosphere of *All's Well that Ends Well* is quite different. This story comes ultimately (i.e., by way of an Elizabethan translation in Painter's *Palace of Pleasure*) from Boccaccio's *Decameron* (III, 9). Boccaccio wrote some magnificent Courtly Love poems that filtered through to Shakespeare by way of Chaucer's *Knight's Tale* and *Troilus and Criseyde*, which are based on them, but the decorum of the *Decameron* demands a different approach. There Boccaccio shows little interest in the ennobling and creative aspects of love, but he is never tired of insisting that the attitude of the church and established society to the sexual needs of young people is dismally unrealistic and uncomprehending. Boccaccio's story in its turn is related to well-known folktale themes, such as the healing of the impotent king and the clever heroine who, like Psyche in Apuleius, somehow manages to accomplish impossible tasks.

To sketch in the setting of the play: a great doctor has died before the play begins, leaving his daughter Helena, the heroine of the play, an orphan, and leaving behind him also a number of recipes for curing diseases that apparently have practically supernatural powers. Helena is adopted into the household of the Countess of Rousillon, where she falls in love with the Countess' son Bertram. The news spreads that the king of France is ill of a disease that has baffled his doctors, so that he has given up hope of a cure. Helena feels that if she can get to him she can cure him, and will ask Bertram as a husband for her reward. Bertram has, by his own father's death, become a ward of the king's, hence the marriage, in such circumstances, would normally be easy enough to arrange, whatever her difference in rank from Bertram.

As in the romances especially, Shakespeare seems to emphasize, even to go out of his way to emphasize, the most primitive and archaic folktale aspects of his story. He includes from his source the bargain by which Helena offers to suffer death by torture if she fails, though accepting such a proposal, as the king appears to do by implication, seems rather out of key with his character. Shakespeare adds to his source a strong emphasis on the fact that the king is not merely healed but rejuvenated, including apparently the restoring of his sexual activity. It seems clear that Helena's healing powers, in which she has such complete confidence, are really a form of magic, whatever she may have found in her father's recipe-books. If so, perhaps the rather puzzling dialogue at the beginning between Helena and Parolles about the former's virginity, often attributed to a corrupt text, may be emphasizing the traditional folktale association of magic with virgins. So if Helena succeeds in her design of marrying Bertram she will also be, like most magicians in plays, renouncing her magic at the end.

In any case she claims her reward, of marriage to Bertram, who will have nothing to do with her, and although he does go through a wedding ceremony under compulsion, he leaves immediately and tells her she can expect nothing from him as a husband. He puts this in the riddling form so common in folktales: she will have to bear a son by a husband who refuses to sleep with her and wear an ancestral ring of his that never comes off his hand. The device employed here is worth an extra comment. In a story by Edgar Allan Poe, *Three Sundays in a Week*, the narrator is told by a crusty uncle that he cannot marry the girl of his choice until three Sundays come together in a week. The solution is along the lines of Jules Verne's *Round the World in Eighty Days*, which was doubtless derived from it. In the course of the story the narrator remarks that his uncle had no qualms about breaking the spirit of one of his vows, but the letter was inviolate. This is exactly the principle that impossible-task folktales operate on, because these riddling conditions can always be broken in the letter. So as soon as we hear Bertram's refusal couched in these terms, we know that he has no chance of getting away with his refusal.

Bertram's hostile reaction, like Isabella's to Claudio's pleading, does not make him a very attractive figure to the audience, but, like Isabella again, his attitude is comprehensible enough in itself. Admittedly he is, like Isabella, emotionally immature, though far less intelligent than she, and everything in his male ego is disgusted by the situation. Women are not to choose but to be chosen; Bertram does not want to marry and 'settle down,' but to become a soldier and have dashing affairs, and even if he did marry he wouldn't want someone he had previously thought of as something between a kid sister and a family retainer. He resents (though in his society he would have had to suppress this anyway) the fact that both his mother and the king think that marriage would be good for him. More important than any of this, the king is fulfilling a promise made to Helena about which he was never consulted, and is making his life and interests only the means of doing so. However benevolent everyone's intentions may be, Bertram sees the whole pattern of his life snatched away from him just at the moment that he is about to enter on it. To put the matter within the central metaphor of our present concerns, he is not ready to see the current of his life suddenly reversed.

Helena is not so easily balked. She is no goddess for all her magic, but a warm-hearted and impulsive young woman whose affection for Bertram has outrun her discretion. Hence while Bernard Shaw may regard her as a proto-Ibsenite, Boccaccio, and Painter more explicitly, merely think of her prototype as a bit pushy. Shakespeare himself puts her through the concealments and disguises that his heroines so often resort to. He does not dress her up as a boy this time, only as a pilgrim, but he also uses, as he does with so many heroines, the pretence that she is dead. The heroine in Shakespearean comedy often brings about the comic resolution by her own efforts, but she never has quite the role of a deputy dramatist. The conventions of the time demand that she keep the lowest possible profile, of which the bed trick and the rumoured death are about as explicit symbols as one could get.

Bertram wishes to seduce a virtuous young woman named Diana, and Helena persuades Diana to seem to agree but allow Helena to replace her in the actual assignation. Meanwhile, Bertram greatly admires a *miles gloriosus* figure named Parolles, and the parallel between Bertram and Parolles is central to the structure of the play. We saw previously that each of the problem plays has a compulsive talker who specializes in slander, the socially disintegrating use of words, the opposite pole of the union of love and eloquence that we met in the *Phaedrus*. Bertram, besides not being in love, is about as inarticulate as any major character in Shakespeare, but Parolles, as his name suggests, is at no loss for words in any situation, except for the one moment when he believes his captors to be Russians and says 'And I must lose my life for want of language.' This scene, in which he is blindfolded and then exposed as a coward by the other officers, runs parallel to Bertram's assignation, for Bertram, if not actually blindfolded, is as much hoodwinked in the dark by the bed trick as though he were. The exuberant flow of the slanders of the terrified Parolles arouses some amused admiration even among the officers against whom they are directed, and however self-defeating his performance, it has more *brio* than Bertram's shufflings and evasions with the king in the recognition scene that corresponds to it.

Some characters in the play, notably Lafeu, express the view that Parolles is really Bertram's evil genius, but, as Lafeu himself soon comes to recognize, Parolles will not sustain such a role: he may be a fool but he is not really malignant. Even his rhyming letter to Diana, which is intercepted by the officers, warning her against Bertram, may be more well-intended than treacherous, however inept. His importance in the play is of a different kind. In most of Shakespeare's comedies the social ranks and relationships are unchanged by the action of the play: *All's Well* is almost the only play in which there is an explicit social promotion in the foreground of the action – and I say 'almost' only because of the 'preposterous estate' of the shepherds at the end of *The Winter's Tale*. It is emphasized that Helena is below Bertram in social status, and that it takes direct intervention of the king to make her marriage possible. Such a theme introduces the conception of one's 'natural place' in society, the position for which one is fitted by one's talents and social function.

Parolles pretends to be a captain, and greatly resents being called Bertram's follower or servant. But he discovers, like others of his type, that his will to survive is stronger than his commitment to heroism. The heightening of experience through love, creativity, or heroism is not for him: he has to fall back on *eros* at its minimum level, the level where it is only the mechanical impulse to keep life going. 'Simply the thing I am / Shall make me live.' In his society that means that he has to accept a social demotion and look around for a master. Apart from Bertram, everybody has talked to him, even Helena, as though he were a fool or clown, and it is apparently in that role that he is accepted into Lafeu's train at the end. His soliloquy, from which the above quotation is taken, ends with a burst of self-confidence: the contrast between that and his later appearance before Lafeu suggests that he had a much rougher time in between than the action of the play itself indicates. That gives to his superficially farcical role a dimension of self-discovery that makes it considerably more serious.

In any case, Parolles adopts the normal direction of life, but at least he knows that he is doing it. An officer eavesdropping on him, when he is cursing himself for talking too much, says: 'is it possible he should know what he is, and be what he is?' One would think that this was eminently possible for everybody: self-knowledge does not necessarily lead to improved action, though it does for him once he is out of his false role. Bertram, with his effort to prove his virility by trying to seduce Diana, is in the opposite situation of self-will without self-knowledge. A comment on Bertram by another officer makes this clear: 'He that in this action contrives against his own nobility, in his proper stream o'erflows himself.' The overflowing 'proper stream' is a modulation of the central theme of the play. Bertram's current of life and energy is flowing the wrong way, which is also, like the descent to hell in *Aeneid*, the easy way. *All's Well* does not have the explicit link with the Bible that *Measure for Measure* indicates in its title, but the Biblical connection is there, and it comes out in an apocalyptic speech by the clown Lavache, perhaps the most extraordinary speech by a clown in the whole of Shakespeare: 'I am for the house with the narrow gate ... but the many will be ... for the flow'ry way that leads to the broad gate and great fire.' He also says that those that 'humble themselves' may go in the opposite direction, and a humbling process is in store for Bertram as well as Parolles, along with a reversal of his energy.

In the recognition scene Bertram, after being caught out in all his lies, finally disgorges one couplet indicating that he has accepted the situation, is willing to take on Helena as his wife, and in general do as he has been told. The couplet says:

> If she, my liege, can make to know this clearly,
> I'll love her dearly, ever, ever dearly.

The speech does not pierce us with its passion, and, with its 'if,' would not win any prizes for gallantry either. But consider Bertram's situation. He has been wrung dry by being processed through a Shakespearean recognition scene, and an instant earlier has been under arrest on suspicion of having murdered his wife. More important for our present point of view, he is, in every conceivable sense of the word, all turned around. He has strained every muscle, so to speak, to travel east, and finds that he has been going west the whole time. The woman he thought he was running away from he turns out to have slept with, and she has the ring he knew he gave to someone else. He can get his bearings only by accepting the direction in which he is actually facing, which he naturally does, like Parolles, with reluctance and bewilderment.

If his surrender lacks enthusiasm, it is still enough to justify the title of the play, which Helena has already repeated twice, and the king a third time in the epilogue. For 'All's Well that Ends Well,' the only title in Shakespeare with a predicate, is a statement only about the structure of comedy, and is mere nonsense as a statement about human life. The reason why it is true of comedy is that when a comedy 'ends well,' the ending is traditionally the beginning of the real lives of the more sympathetic characters. Bertram has not shown much capacity to love, but according to comic convention he will later. So, again, the reversal of Bertram's libido from war and lechery to genuine life illustrates a myth of deliverance, in the form of redemption, and, once more, illustrates it within the context of comedy. In the hands of a second-rate dramatist it would be only a mirror of the audience's ready-made conceptions of such things: it would be, that is, a sentimental melodrama in which a young man going to the dogs is redeemed by the self-sacrificing love of a noble young woman. In Shakespeare's hands it has all possible comic dimensions, including the ironic dimension which has made so many critics of the play feel uncomfortable, much as Lafeu is made uncomfortable by Lavache's gloomy prophecy.

In *All's Well*, then, there is the current of self-wasting energy that I have called the Eros-Thanatos current, symbolized by Bertram's self-will, Parolles' lack of heroism, and Lavache's vision of the great mass of people drifting to the 'broad gate and the great fire.' There is also the reversal of this current of energy backward into a renewed and creative life. The play opens with older characters 'all in black,' talking mainly about the dead; it proceeds through the healing of an impotent king to a recognition scene which is largely an inquest on the alleged death of Helena. Helena rejuvenates the family, the king, and may even rejuvenate Bertram's fixated notions of family honour and tradition. As in *Measure for Measure*, many of the central characters are brought very close to an actual confrontation with death. Helena explicitly risks her life on the success of her healing of the king, spreads a rumour that she has actually died, and thereby forces Bertram to face the possibility of a death sentence. Parolles is told when blindfolded that he is going to be hanged after all, a farcical suggestion to us but hardly to him.

Yet, again as in *Measure for Measure*, nobody gets permanently hurt in the long run, and, in a world where the principle of 'all's well that ends well' is true, that is what matters. The central bed trick device seems to be, once again, an image of passage through death to new life, a passion-motivated descent into an illusion that reverses itself and turns to reality and renewed energy. Angelo and Bertram are quite sure that they want specific women, Isabella and Diana, and not others, Mariana and Helena, but their lust in the dark takes no account of what they think they want. We notice that the reversal of Bertram's (and Angelo's) current of libido is not a sublimation in any Platonic or Freudian sense. It is what might be called the fundamental sublimation, the movement from what is traditionally called lust to what is traditionally called true love, initiated by the woman but to be later completed by the man. In lust we have an instinctive and generalized desire of *a* man for *a* woman (or vice versa), which cannot rise above the genital union to include personality, friendship, or tenderness. The wars Bertram is engaged in are obviously not very bloody, but accessible if not necessarily willing women are supposed to be a perquisite of the soldier's death-dealing trade. Bertram does not want to kill Diana, but he does want to turn her into a sexual object he will not even have to like or respect, much less love, and that would destroy her integrity as a woman quite as effectively. There is such a thing as a fate worse than death: this dimension of the action is very lightly touched in the play, but, as with Parolles, there are suggestions of something more serious in the background of the action.

The dawn of the conventional true love, and the uniting of such love through all obstacles, was the central theme of most comedy for two thousand years, and in fact still is, though the myriads of examples of it that continue to appear (even in a society where so large a proportion of marriages either end in divorce or endure in misery) are for the most part ignored in university classrooms. The vision of a newborn society centred on love, which is whisked away from us by the end of the play, remains in our minds as the core of the desperate hope that the natural cycle will one day turn from winter to summer, from darkness to dawn, from aged impotence to youthful energy, from the heroism of murder to the heroism of social life, and then stop. As Helena says:

> But with the word the time will bring on summer,
> When briars shall have leaves as well as thorns
> And be as sweet as sharp. We must away;
> Our wagon is prepared, and time revives us.
> All's well that ends well: still the fine's the crown.

If Helena's 'word' is specifically the word 'yet,' which she has just used twice, she is speaking of the comic resolution at the end, which the audience carries away with them as a vision projected on the future, which has nevertheless been 'presented' as the one vision that humanity wants to become present.

In some respects *All's Well* is not typical of Shakespeare's usual practice in constructing comedies. The typical New Comedy plot that we have so often referred to, which came to Renaissance Europe mainly from Plautus and Terence, features the victory of the young over the old, with two young people getting married in spite of the opposition of their parents. It often featured too, within limits, the triumph of a tricky slave who takes the side of the young hero and outwits the *senex* figure. Often the slave is freed or the heroine is proved to be of noble birth. The imagery is mainly social, and while such a form can hardly be called revolutionary, within an authoritarian society it affords a good deal of psychological release. Shakespeare adopts many New Comedy features, but his main focus is less on social than on natural and sexual images of renewed fertility. The social ranks established at the beginning of the play are normally unchanged at the end, and he seems to dislike the tricky slave role. Puck and Ariel are elemental spirits acting under orders, and his clever servants remain only that.

But *All's Well* has a much more restless feeling of social change about it, with Bertram being pulled out of the clichés of family pride in the direction of Helena's still mysterious capacities, Helena herself advancing from the background of the Rousillon household to a primary place in it, the clown Lavache turning philosophical, and the captain Parolles becoming a licensed fool in Lafeu's train. It does not, we said, suggest as many analogies to Christian conceptions as *Measure for Measure* does, but, especially in Lavache's oracular speech, there is a faint whisper of the vision of social reversal that finds expression in the Magnificat: 'he has put down the mighty from their seats, and exalted them of low degree.' The king remains the king, of course, but when the actor playing him goes out to ask for the audience's applause, his opening line is 'The king's a beggar, now the play is done.' *Measure for Measure*, where the main emphasis is on the return and restoration of the original Duke's authority, is more typical of Shakespeare's comic structures. But when we take the two problem comedies together, we get a greatly expanded vision of comic themes and possibilities.

In *Measure for Measure* the two halves of the action illustrate a dialectic between life and art, in which the elaborate dramaturgy of the disguised Duke reverses and redeems the direction of life for all the characters. The implication is that art redeems the past by separating what is creative in it from the general death-wish frenzy of ordinary history. Every work of art was produced in history, and was therefore contemporary with the usual amount of human folly, injustice, destructiveness, and cruelty; but the work of art itself seems to retain an odd quality of innocence. This quality of innocence is, or is closely connected with, its power to communicate with future generations. The unquenchable human hope for more peace and justice in the future, which the triumph of youth in a typical New Comedy action symbolizes, complements this feeling. Thus if a creative artist (we may think for example of William Morris in the nineteenth century) becomes deeply committed to social movements intended to bring about a better society in the future, he is not being inconsistent if he is also committed, quite as strongly, to preserving and continuing the creativity of a distant past.

These comments may seem to be taking us a long way from the problem comedies, but they are not so far from the great romances that follow them in Shakespeare's canon. We noted that the diptych construction of *Measure for Measure* reappears in *The Winter's Tale*, where in a clearly marked place a switch from blank verse to prose heralds the beginning of a new action. But the new life and deliverance to which the action of *The Winter's Tale* leads seems to go in two quite different, if complementary, directions. One direction is the marriage of Florizel and Perdita, which evades parental opposition in typical New Comedy fashion, by demonstrating that Perdita is a real princess. The imagery of this resolution is connected with the renewal of nature. Its focus is in the great sheep-shearing festival of the fourth act, where there are flowers for every season of the year, including winter-flowers for the disguised Polixenes and Camillo, who act as spirits of frost and snow, trying to destroy the festivity, in which they have little permanent success, however great the temporary confusion they cause. The triumph of youth over age is attached to such images as covering Florizel 'like a corse' with flowers, and with Perdita's total rejection of any floral product of nature in which art has had a share. Florizel's former tricky servant, Autolycus, has a most important role in this scene, but it is not the typical New Comedy plot-role of helping to bring about the festive ending for the young people. He would rather like such a role, but, consistently with Shakespeare's usual attitude to such figures, the recognition takes place without him.

The recognition scene itself is reported only, in the conversation of some gentlemen, and in rather stilted language at that. It is clearly being subordinated to another recognition scene which occupies the conclusion of the play. This is the meeting of Leontes with Hermione, the imagery of which is a contrast in every way to its counterpart. Its theme is not a new marriage of young people with happiness predicated for the future, but the healing of a breach in the past and the reconciling of a middle-aged couple. The imagery is not of the coming of spring and the renewing force of nature without reference to art; the meeting takes place in a building (Paulina's chapel), where all the arts are referred to. Leontes is presented with what is alleged to be a work of painting and sculpture, and the name of an actual and well-known artist (Julio Romano) is attached to it, which seems curious, as, on the main narrative line presented to us, there is no statue at all. (There are, of course, other narrative lines, in which Hermione is rising from the dead or emerging from the statue like Galatea.) Music and poetry are employed in the final awakening of Hermione, and there are references to magic, which was a common meaning of the word 'art' at the time.

In *The Tempest* there is a similar double resolution. Ferdinand and Miranda are to be married and enter their brave new world, and parental opposition is minimized: that of Alonso is passed over and that of Prospero only simulated. Prospero makes quite a fuss over preserving Miranda's virginity until the marriage rites have been completed, but that is again less a matter of morality than of magic. As in all magic, timing is of the essence of the operation, and without proper timing the marriage will not have the fertility promised in the masque. Meanwhile Prospero himself has settled accounts with the enemies in his past: that is, reconciliation and forgiveness have closed up what Leontes, at the end of *The Winter's Tale*, calls 'this great gap of time.' So once more there is a healing of the past through art (here represented by Prospero's magic, which however includes the dramatic and musical art of the masque), and a projection of future happiness for the young lovers through the natural energies personified in the masque as Juno, the sky, Ceres, the earth, and Iris, the rainbow. The implication seems to be that the central resolution of the comedy is something in a present where past and future are gathered, in Eliot's phrase, which combines these two tonalities in an overall harmony.

It has been suggested that the action of *The Tempest*, in moving from North Africa through an enchanted island to Italy, is designed to recall the journey of Aeneas from Carthage through the Sibyl's cave to Latium, and the suggestion seems to me obviously right. What Aeneas sees in the lower world is a vision of a historical future. The historical future in *The Tempest* is not obvious; but every editor of the play is compelled to deal in his introduction with the pamphlets and other documents that Shakespeare used about voyages across the Atlantic to the New World, in spite of the fact that the play itself never goes outside the Mediterranean Sea. Perhaps in the background we can see a vast historical cycle turning from the Renaissance Magus with his elemental spirits to a future of colonizing and exploring in a new world that will generate new ideas about the natural man and natural societies, along the lines begun by Montaigne's essay on the cannibals, another source for *The Tempest*. This is not a comic perspective, of course, nor does it suggest any myth of deliverance, but is simply the wheel of history continuing to revolve. Still, it raises larger questions about art and nature and the relation of both to reality and illusion. To this final aspect of reversal and recognition we must now turn.

3

The Reversal of Reality

TWO OF SHAKESPEARE'S PROBLEM PLAYS, then, are fairly typical comedies in which redemptive forces are set to work that bring about the characteristic festive conclusion, the birth of a new society, that gives to the audience the feeling that 'everything's going to be all right after all.' Such plays illustrate what we have been calling the myth of deliverance, a sense of energies released by forgiveness and reconciliation, where Eros triumphs over Nomos or law, by evading what is frustrating or absurd in law and fulfilling what is essential for social survival. But comedy is a mixture of the festive and the ironic, of a drive toward a renewed society along with a strong emphasis on the arbitrary whims and absurdities that block its emergence. There is a much larger infusion of irony in *Measure for Measure* and *All's Well* than in, say, *As You Like It* or *Twelfth Night*, and of course there are many comedies, especially in modern times, where the ironic emphasis is too strong for the drive toward deliverance, and where the play ends in frustration and blocked movement. In Shakespeare's canon the play that comes nearest to this is *Troilus and Cressida*, a play that, whatever else it may do, does not illustrate the myth of deliverance in comedy. It seems to be designed rather to show us human beings getting into the kind of mess that requires deliverance, a secular counterpart of what Christianity calls the fall of man.

Shakespeare's plays are classified by the Folio as comedies, tragedies, and histories, to which modern critics generally add romance as a fourth genre. *Troilus and Cressida* is hard to 'fit into' these categories (I use quotation marks because 'fitting' is not the point of generic criticism) because it has so many elements of all four. It is a kind of history play, for the Trojan War was the normal beginning of secular history in Shakespeare's day, and the characters in it sometimes seem to realize that they are establishing the patterns and types of the future. The most obvious example is the scene (III, ii) in which Troilus, Cressida, and Pandarus successively speak as it were to the future, a posterity who will take Troilus to be the pattern of truth and fidelity, Cressida the pattern of falseness, if she proves false, Pandarus to be the patron saint of all panders.

Again, the Troilus story was not part of the Homer-Virgil account: it was the medieval romance precipitate, so to speak, of the Trojan War, and came to Shakespeare from medieval sources, notably Chaucer. Shakespeare's warriors, especially the Trojans, are almost completely medievalized, and fight according to the romantic medieval codes of chivalry and Courtly Love. The strongly anti-Greek tone of the play is also derived from the fact that medieval Europe was sympathetic to the Trojans because of Virgil's story that the Trojans had founded Rome. This story was adapted to Britain by Geoffrey of Monmouth, whose legendary history, with its suggestion that Britain was to be a third great Trojan kingdom succeeding Rome, was widely accepted in Shakespeare's day, appearing in Spenser's *Faerie Queene* and elsewhere.

The play also seems to be a tragedy, what with the death of Hector, the destruction of Troilus' trust by Cressida, and the bitter final scene, with Troy approaching its final catastrophe. Yet the author of the curious epistle to the reader which prefaces the reprinted Quarto regards it as a comedy, though he realizes that it is a very black comedy, and unlikely to find a warm response in the public theatre. He suggests that it was not acted in Shakespeare's lifetime: there is other evidence that it was, but it could hardly have been a popular play then. It is generally recognized, however, that it is a uniquely 'modern' play, with its ambiguous irony, its learned language, and the prominence it gives to the anti-heroic. For the same reason the twentieth century has less difficulty in placing it within the comic context.

The play seems to revolve around the relation of reality and illusion. In the conference of Trojan leaders (II, ii) the association of fame and glory and the like with the rape of Helen, and the attempt to make that rape seem more glamorous by persisting in fighting for it, is recognized by Hector to be pure illusion, and even Troilus, though he asks 'What's aught but as 'tis valued?,' understands this too. The Trojans, then, choose the illusion of fame and glory, knowing it to be an illusion, and knowing that Helen herself is not the real motive for fighting. In Euripides' play on Helen a version of the legend is adopted in which the Helen who was in Troy during the war was a wraith or illusion, the real Helen being in Egypt the whole time. The very commonplace and minor Helen of Shakespeare's play is not a ghost, but the fact that she is as little worth all that bloodshed as though she were seems to be patent to everyone. Later, when Troilus is forced to watch as Cressida takes up with the Greek Diomed, a similar problem arises in his mind. Which is the real Cressida, the one deserting to the Greeks or the faithful one who was an essential part of his own identity?

The Greeks, though caught up in the same fantasy, are, by comparison, realists. Ulysses makes an impressive speech on the chain of being and the fact that society depends on hierarchical order, in order to suggest that Achilles, who is a 'better' warrior than anyone present, should be brought back into the conflict. The appeal to the chain of being undercuts the personal application, but there is also some expert needling of Agamemnon and Nestor in Ulysses' description of the way in which Achilles ridicules them to Patroclus. The proposal modulates into a scheme of replacing Achilles with Ajax as the number one Greek hero, which should provoke Achilles to re-enter the combat. This scheme is a kind of controlled experiment within a tragic framework: if we disturb the hierarchy of nature by placing Ajax above Achilles, the disturbance is bound to right itself by the return of Achilles.

The scheme is clever, and up to a point it works, but the real outcome of the play has very little to do with Ulysses' plans, and nothing at all to do with the chain of being. It seems to be assumed in the play that Hector is, in fair fight, invincible, and that neither Ajax nor Achilles would be a match for him. It also seems to be assumed that the murder of Hector, not any hanky-panky with a wooden horse, is what really brings about the fall of Troy. Hector, the knight *sans peur et sans reproche*, who fights without hatred or envy, and is incapable of treachery or malice, is the one moral reality in the play, and he is in the centre of illusion. He agrees to go on fighting, because, as with Othello, it is his occupation or identity; but he fights in a world where sooner or later hatred, malice, and treachery will take over, and wolves will pull down the stag.

If Ulysses believed his own speech about hierarchy and degree, then, he would advise the Greek army to go away and leave Troy in peace. Without degree, he says, everything meets in 'mere oppugnancy,' but what else is the Trojan war? In a state of war, authority must come to terms with the fact that the great majority of fighters are motivated by hatred, and that hatred sooner or later makes use of weapons that, in Thersites' phrase, 'proclaim barbarism' and bring about the chaos that Ulysses pretends to dread.

Thersites, though he has not heard the speech, knows that Ulysses' counsel accomplishes very little as such: 'now is the cur Ajax prouder than the cur Achilles, and will not arm today.' It is particularly in the relations of Ajax and Achilles that we see how heroism is, in Heidegger's term, 'ecstatic,' outside itself, thrown into situations in which the personality recreates itself to meet each one differently. We first see Ajax as a sullen brute whom the Greek leaders manipulate with contemptuous ease, in contrast to Achilles, who is far more intelligent, and, for all his self-indulgence, not ill-natured. But the manipulation does change the personality, and by IV, v, the scene of Hector's visit to the Greek tents, it is Achilles who has become the brute and Ajax who is speaking with moderation and point. The manipulation is too efficient, in other words, to accomplish its own real aim.

We remarked that each of the problem plays has a character who is a focus for slander and railing, the socially irresponsible use of words. This character type is represented in *Troilus and Cressida* by Thersites, but, while the slanders of Lucio and Parolles are the wildest fantasy, the railing of Thersites is close to the facts. The Greek leaders, or some of them, are as stupid as he says they are: the war really is being fought for a whore and a cuckold. Thersites is frustrated by the fact that words do nothing to alter a situation: in fact they cannot even express it. To call Menelaus an ass does not begin to express the stupidity of Menelaus, or the damage such stupidity does in the world. He talks of studying magic in order to give some effectiveness to his curses, but in the mean time all his vituperation cannot evoke the irony that the Prologue achieves with the baldest of factual statements:

The ravished Helen, Menelaus' queen,
With wanton Paris sleeps; and that's the quarrel.

Still, Thersites' function is significant: the slanders of Lucio and
Parolles illustrate how the irresponsible use of words tends to dis-
integrate society, but the railing of Thersites brings out the element of self-delusion in the rhetoric of the warriors.

Every history play of Shakespeare makes it clear that, in the art
of ruling, Plato's philosopher-king would be an impossible schizo-
phrenic. If a king ever stopped to philosophize, he would lose the
rhythm of action on which his effectiveness as a ruler depends.
Similarly, in this play it is the primacy of the will which is con-
stantly stressed: the will is there to act, and knowledge and reason
have very little function beyond a purely tactical one. Continuity
of action is therefore not necessarily consistency of action: one
responds to the situation that is there, however different it may be
from the previous one. There is no reason to doubt the genuine-
ness of Cressida's affection for Troilus as long as Troilus is present;
but when Diomed is present she rationalizes her desertion of
Troilus by speaking of the way in which sense perception of the
immediate takes control over the shadows of memory.

The great Hindu scripture, the *Bhagavadgita*, is an episode from
a heroic epic, the *Mahabharata*, in which two bands of warrior
nobles face one another in battle, and a warrior on one side,
Arjuna, wonders why he should be fighting an army which con-
tains so many of his own relatives. Similarly, the Greeks and
Trojans are more closely related than one might at first expect: the
Helen known throughout history as Helen of Troy is the wife of a
Greek warrior; her abduction is said to be retaliation for the pre-
vious abduction of the Trojan Hesione, who was given to a Greek;
Cressida follows her deserting father into the Greek camp; Hector

will not risk killing Ajax because Ajax is half Trojan; Achilles' professed reason for abandoning the battle is that he is secretly in love with a daughter of Priam. Arjuna is told by his charioteer, the god Krishna in disguise, to stay and fight because he is a warrior and should fight, and Hector, we saw, agrees in the Trojan council to go on fighting although he knows there is no real reason for doing so. Arjuna is finally rewarded by a vision of the universe within the body of the god Krishna, but in *Troilus and Cressida* we get no such vision, only Ulysses' speeches about the necessity of degree and the oblivion connected with time.

These speeches are partly sepia clouds concealing much more practical aims, but they have a dramatic function far beyond that. They are, in fact, speeches about the two bases of what we think of as reality: about our perception of time and space, space being presented as the hierarchical structure familiar to Shakespeare's audience and time as the devouring monster equally familiar from the sonnets and elsewhere. Ulysses' function in the play is not that of a warrior but of a counsellor, and his speeches represent the detachment of intelligence from the rest of consciousness (rather like Falstaff's speech on honour, in a less farcical context), leaving the warriors to fight with a ferocity untroubled by the calls of the intellect.

When we look at these speeches in the context of the play, the presiding geniuses of space and time appear to be Tantalus and Sisyphus. The imagery of the opening lines of the play speaks of 'tarrying,' waiting endlessly for something not yet to be grasped, and before long Cressida is telling us that this is in fact part of her own strategy to 'hold off.' Men, she says, concentrate on women only as long as they are out of reach: once the women are possessed, the men revert to their former interests. As she says bitterly after her first night with Troilus:

You men will never tarry.
O foolish Cressid! I might have still held off,
And then you would have tarried.

However, she is soon moved to a Greek context, where what is appropriate is not to hold off but to hold on. The theme of tantalizing also appears in the emphasis on voyeurism of various kinds, in Pandarus' leering stage-management of the union of the lovers, in Thersites' sardonic comments while watching the seduction of Cressida and Troilus' duel with Diomed, and, on a much more pathetic level, Troilus' involuntary spying on Cressida's unfaithfulness.

The theme of spying appears again in the fact that Troilus' love-affair with Cressida, and Achilles' with a daughter of Priam, are Courtly Love amours where, conventionally, the first requisite is secrecy, yet both affairs are, it seems, well known to the leaders in the two camps. Achilles expresses surprise that his amour is known, and Ulysses, as usual, refers him to the cosmos, with an eloquent speech about the omniscience of 'the providence that's in a watchful state.' He passes over the fact that what watchful providence really knows is that Achilles' alleged love for a daughter of Priam is a coverup for his homosexual infatuation with Patroclus.

Similarly, the speech on time which Ulysses has just delivered to Achilles is a kind of eulogy of Sisyphus, an insistence, not merely that men have short memories, but that envy and self-interest shorten them still further, to the point at which incessant repetitive activity is necessary to sustain one's reputation. It is hardly possible, in such a context, that Sisyphus could be, in Camus' phrase, a happy man: as one's reputation grows, and as continuous effort is needed to sustain it, one finds the stone getting heavier each time it is rolled up the hill.

The speeches of Ulysses define the nature of what Christianity calls a fallen world. We guide ourselves in that world by our perception of time and space, which we perceive in such a way as to make them sources of external authority as well. The cosmos is a world of 'degree'; time is an inexorable wheel of fortune. They are what we have of reality, and produce in us a sense of ineluctable fatality. But no sooner have they done this than they begin to suggest a sense of unreality as well. We noted earlier that Hector and Troilus deliberately choose the illusions of fame and love and glory, knowing them to be illusions. This is of course particularly true of Hector, who talks less about the chain of degree than Ulysses but clearly knows at least as much about it. Yet their decision arouses a response in us that is not only sympathy but a faint perception of a reality that all our metaphysical chains of bondage cannot quite hold in. The inference is that no serious view of life can get established until we have recognized a quality of illusion in what we think of as objective reality, and a quality of reality in what we think of as subjective illusion.

In ordinary experience, what we call real tends to be associated with the objective, with what other people see more or less as we see. What we call illusion is correspondingly associated with the subjective, the world of dream and of the emotions, ranging from love to hatred, that distort our 'real' perspective. It is here, perhaps, that a man of the theatre might have something to say. For Shakespeare was a man of the theatre who concentrated intensely on the theatrical experience: we may even say that in every play he wrote the central character is the theatre itself. When we are in a theatre, the play we see and hear on the stage is, we say, an illusion. But we could search the wings and dressing-rooms forever without finding any reality 'behind' it: it seems clear that in a theatre the illusion *is* the reality. Furthermore, it is as objective a datum as anything else that we see and hear. Whatever is not the play in the theatre is the shared experience of the audience watching it, an experience that will differ with each member of the audience, and yet represents a consensus as well. In a theatre, then, the illusion is objective and the reality subjective. That does not, by itself, completely reverse the nature of reality and illusion, but it suggests that there are other aspects of both to which the drama is relevant.

We notice that something like a reality-illusion distinction is often incorporated into the action of the plays themselves. In the great sequence of historical plays from *Richard II* to *Henry V*, we begin with Richard II, a king so unrealistic in his extravagance and irresponsibility that society's need for real leadership throws up Bolingbroke to fill the vacuum that society as well as nature abhors. Bolingbroke is neither a ruthless usurper nor a puppet pushed forward by others: he is simply the kind of figure who must appear in so troubled a time. He is therefore a practical man taking short views, and that is what enables him to hold power. Everything he does is thrown outwards into the immediate situation, while Richard becomes increasingly narcissistic. The great fortress of extroverted and spontaneous action is our everyday existence in time and space, which we never see objectively without the aid of clocks and mirrors. The growing prominence of these images in Richard's deposition indicates, it seems, his growing assimilation to a subjective and withdrawn world. Similarly, Ulysses' invocation of the chain of being as a gigantic mirror which ought to reflect the Greek army's true shape, and of time as a striking clock which ticks away Achilles' former achievements into oblivion, illustrates the world of divided consciousness that the Trojan War symbolizes.

Bolingbroke's coming to the throne, however inevitable, was still a usurpation, and it left a dark land full of the meteors and comets of rebellion. In the midst of this dark world is the East-cheap tavern with Falstaff and Prince Henry. Almost at once Falstaff speaks of going by the 'moon and the seven stars,' and later calls himself and his companions 'Diana's foresters, gentlemen of the shade, minions of the moon' – language with a grotesque recall of the fairy world of *A Midsummer Night's Dream*. Prince Henry, however, is biding his time: he will eventually 'imitate the sun,' and when he is a king a new day will dawn. The day dawns at the end of *Henry* IV Part Two, when the prince is crowned as Henry V, and, as his first act, destroys the identity of Falstaff, who for a moment clings to the hope that he will 'be sent for at night.' But there is no night in the blazing noon of Henry's conquest of France, except, of course, for France itself. Henry progresses from victory to marriage, after which the wheel of fortune turns once more and England is plunged into another night. The issue involved in the rejection of Falstaff is not a moral one, but the end of a dramatic conflict between Henry's day world of warfare and Falstaff's night world of thieves and whores. Falstaff's world is a world of illusory values, but it is also, dramatically, as intensely real as anything we have in literature. Henry's world is real too, but by no means *the* real world: it is a carefully selected slice of reality, shot through with the illusions inspired by fortune and victory.

Shakespeare's profoundest treatment of the paradox of reality and illusion in history is perhaps *Antony and Cleopatra*. It is easy to approach this play, conventionally, with the assumption that the Roman world represents reality and the Egyptian world illusion, and that Antony loses his grip on reality as a potential world-ruler in exchange for the illusions of Cleopatra's magic. But Cleopatra has not uttered six lines before we realize that any such conception of her is all wrong. She is no Circe-like enchantress and has no illusions at her command. Antony and other

Romans may sometimes call her or think of her as a witch, but it is the luminous daylight reality of the woman 'whom everything becomes' that fascinates Antony and upstages everyone else within reach. Caesar wins the world, but Antony remains a bigger man than Caesar because he is destroyed by a bigger world than Caesar ever knew, and perhaps one more real than any world that can be ruled.

We are beginning to suspect that such collisions of forces in Shakespeare are not collisions of reality and illusion, but collisions of different worlds, each of which has its own form of reality and of illusion. In *Troilus and Cressida* we get a vision of the world that a pro-Trojan reader might well make out of the *Iliad*, a world where all purpose seems perverted and all ideals merely enchantments. Virgil, we saw, reversed the Homeric story into a story of a new Troy that in the course of centuries came to rule over Greece as well. This reversal of heroic action, we also noted, involved a rigid separation between the social concern of warfare and the individual concern of love, and the supremacy of the former over the latter. It has much the same framework as Ulysses' vision of restored degree, with an invincible Achilles detached from the arms of Patroclus, but it has a more positive and permanent, in short a more genuinely historical, aim.

A century before Shakespeare another epic portrayal of the conflict of love and war was given in Ariosto's *Orlando Furioso*. In Ariosto's romance there is assumed to be a deeply serious state of warfare at the centre of the Christian world. Paris is under siege by a Saracen or Moslem army, a situation which is a kind of crusade in reverse. Both Christian and Saracen forces are led by individual heroes who keep wandering off on their own mainly erotic affairs and meeting one challenge after another, of a kind to which their chivalric code must give top priority. Ariosto makes it fairly clear that if the Christian heroes would unite they could easily drive off the Saracen army, and that if the Saracen heroes would unite they could easily take Paris. Orlando, the figure corresponding to Achilles in the *Iliad*, is the greatest of the Christian champions, but he has gone mad in pursuit of a Saracen (or at any rate pagan) heroine named Angelica, and has retired from the conflict.

It is a well-known fact that whatever is lost on earth is collected in the moon, that being what the moon is for. If Orlando is mad, he must have lost his wits, and if he has lost his wits they must be somewhere in the moon. So an English knight named Astolfo rides on a 'hippogriff' or flying horse to the top of a high mountain, whence he changes planes to Elijah's chariot of fire to go on to the moon. He is taken on a tour there by St John, and, sure enough, he sees a large bottle labelled 'Orlando's wits.' He takes possession of this, returns to the earth, and pours the contents into Orlando's nose. Orlando immediately recovers his sanity, finds that he no longer cares anything about Angelica, and settles down to help destroy the Saracen army.

If one were to suspect a certain light-heartedness in Ariosto's treatment one would be right, but there is a serious theme behind it all the same. This is brought out in the many references to the distant future of the story which is Ariosto's present, and in which Italy is becoming increasingly the battlefield of stronger invading forces from France and the Empire. So the account of Astolfo's journey to the moon seems to expand into a vision of the moon as a 'lunatic' counterpart of the real world, a world which, except that it exists, is both the source and the repository of all illusion. The vast poem therefore turns on a reversal of the action, from madness to sanity, from the moon to the earth, from ultimately frivolous to ultimately serious concerns, that reminds us in some respects of the crucial return from the lower world in the *Aeneid*. We note that the closing line in Ariosto is modelled on the closing line of the *Aeneid*. But the reversal in the *Aeneid* assumes that

Aeneas has to abandon not only Dido but, so to speak, the whole Dido way of life, and cling to his historical destiny as founder of the Roman Empire. In Ariosto there is rather the feeling that somehow the sane and the lunatic ways of life have to be brought together and put in some kind of alignment before the story is complete.

We are not surprised to find that in Shakespeare's lighter comedies it frequently happens that a world presented dramatically as a 'real' world, full of courts and order and justice and other conventional attributes of reality, is opposed to a fairy-tale world of magic and enchantment, out of which the comic resolution comes. It is, I think, in A Midsummer Night's Dream that we can see this 'green world' type of structure in Shakespearean comedy most fully and suggestively. The action of this play is constructed around three main groupings of its characters. The first group is at the Athenian court, with Theseus and Hippolyta at the centre, and four lovers before them. As so often in comedy, an absurd or unreasonable law is being appealed to, in this case by Hermia's father Egeus. The law of Athens says that a young woman must marry the man her father chooses or face the alternatives of death or perpetual imprisonment in a convent. Egeus is far gone in senility, and shows no distress at the possibility of his daughter's being executed if she does not marry the man he chooses as a surrogate for himself. It is natural to want to rationalize this scene by saying that Theseus probably has a better private strategy in mind, and will talk Egeus around to it offstage. But all we actually hear Theseus say echoes Angelo's 'no remedy': he must and will enforce the law as it stands. We may also perhaps infer from his parenthetical 'What cheer, my love?' that Hippolyta, who is presented throughout as a person of great common sense, is disappointed, if not disgusted, with the situation.

Once again, an unreasonable law, whatever we think of it, is not openly denounced but merely evaporates from the action. It is there to present a state of contrast to the direction in which the comic action moves. In the world where there could be such a law, reason and order are assumed to be in complete control of emotion and impulse, and the most natural symbol of this is absolute parental authority, especially in sexual matters, with any deviation from it leading to death or sterility. Perhaps, if we carried out this conception of reason and order to its logical conclusion, the reality it invokes would turn out to be simply whatever is dead, with illusion the flickering flame of life within it.

In the second grouping we are in the wood of Oberon and Titania, with the Quince company in one corner of it and the four lovers in another. This is a world of magic and metamorphosis and confused identity, and has strong affinities with the world of dream, as the play's title indicates. In this wood there are farcical versions being enacted of two of the world's greatest tragic stories: that of Pyramus and Thisbe by the Quince company, and that of the *Knight's Tale* by the lovers, with two male rivals in pursuit, first of Hermia, and then of Helena. As dawn breaks, Theseus and Hippolyta enter the wood hunting, meet the lovers there, and Theseus quite suddenly reverses his former decision, telling Egeus that he will overbear his will. The conscious or daylight reason for his change of attitude is the switching of Demetrius' affections to Helena. But that was the work of Oberon, whose influence is not, Oberon says, confined only to the hours of darkness. Oberon seems to be something of a deputy dramatist too.

In any case everyone comes together in the third and final arrangement, in a series of concentric circles. Quince's group is in a most unlikely place, at the centre and the focus of attention, the lovers, including Theseus and Hippolyta, being grouped around them. At the end of the scene the human characters retire from the stage, and the fairies come in for the blessing of the house, indicating that the concluding action, though in Theseus' court, is as much under their inspection as the action of the previous night in the wood. If so, there is a very central irony in the fact that the final act begins with Theseus' speech on art dismissing all claims to reality on the part of such spiritual beings as those who have just reversed his authority.

Theseus' famous speech, among its many remarkable features, uses the word 'apprehend' and 'comprehend' twice, in order to make an analogy between ordinary life and art. In ordinary life sense experience apprehends and reason comprehends. Here reason is or should be in charge, and rules out or modifies sense data when they are distorted by excessive emotion. In the dark, sense alone may not be able to distinguish a bush from a bear, but the more frightened one is, the stronger the impulse to think it a bear. The poet's business, however, is to 'apprehend' emotion itself, rather than sense data, and he instantly tries to 'comprehend' it with what a later critic would call an objective correlative to put around it: a symbol, a story framework, character, or whatever:

> Such tricks hath strong imagination
> That if it would but apprehend some joy,
> It comprehends some bringer of that joy.

The emotion of joy is what is 'apprehended'; and then a goddess of Mirth or a lucky accident or a discovered treasure is brought in to 'comprehend' it. In all this Theseus uses the word 'imagination' in its customary Renaissance sense as the tendency to create things that are not there out of the things that are there, illusion out of reality.

Such a theory, consistently with Theseus' social attitude, to law and everything else, makes poetry a form of illusion which must be kept strictly subordinate to reality. When the Quince play is brought to him, Theseus sees what for him is the reality in it, the fact that, whatever its merits, it is a sincere effort to do him honour. As with a modern social critic, the play is primarily for him a reflection of the class structure of his own society. The sensitivity and courtesy with which he responds to the play are genuine enough, and the actors are left with the impression that they have done an excellent job of entertaining the court, as indeed they have. But we may notice that the Quince play is, as Theseus himself says, a 'palpable-gross play' which is almost a parody of Theseus' conception of the imagination.

The actors are sure that the ladies at least in their audience will not be able to distinguish fiction from fact, and so accompany their lion with reassurances that he is not a real lion, along with a talking wall and an ambulatory moonlight. Brecht with all his 'alienating' devices could hardly do better: illusion is entirely subject to the reality of the world the audience normally lives in. The main reason why Quince's players adopt these procedures is that the court is their fairyland. They hardly think of their audiences (or, again, the ladies in it) as real people at all. If Snug the joiner dresses up as a lion, he would be unlikely to be much worried about the reactions of Mrs Snug the joiner, but court ladies are unimaginably delicate and fragile. Theories of reality, it seems, whether they originate in the mind of Theseus or of Peter Quince, do not appear to lead to an overwhelming sense of reality.

When Hippolyta says, voicing the thought that is in everyone's mind, that the play is the silliest stuff she has ever heard, Theseus says:

The best in this kind are but shadows; and the worst are no worse, if imagination amend them.

The remark is not very adequate as dramatic criticism, as it puts William Shakespeare and Peter Quince on much the same level, but when anything is repeated in Shakespeare (as with the words 'apprehend' and 'comprehend' in Theseus' speech) it is likely to be something to look at rather sharply, and Puck's epilogue repeats two of the key words used here:

> If we shadows have offended,
> Think but this, and all is mended,
> That you have but slumbered here.

And when we add the comments of Hippolyta, who has so much more incisive and concrete a mind than Theseus, we get something more interesting.

Hippolyta disagrees with Theseus about the reality of the lovers' experience, but she does not adopt his categories and say that she is inclined to believe it because of its internal consistency. She says rather:

> ... all their minds transfigur'd so together,
> More witnesseth than fancy's images,
> And grows to something of great constancy;
> But howsoever, strange and admirable.

Every drama of Shakespeare contains a great variety of sub-dramas, and the sub-drama of the four lovers in the enchanted wood, however fanciful in detail, is a whole experience which is infinitely greater than the sum of its parts. The word 'transfigur'd' indicates that the experience is neither real nor illusory, but has got clear of that commonplace antithesis. The dramatist is not interested in the credible, but in the strange and admirable, the illusion more real than reality, the reality that incorporates all the dreams of illusion. Hippolyta's other comment is in response to Theseus' remark, quoted above, that all dramas are unreal, and bad plays can be good plays if imagination amend them. She says:

'it must be your imagination then, and not theirs.' Here 'imagination' is approaching its more modern meaning of creative power, and Hippolyta is ascribing the essential imagination in this creative sense to the audience and not to the dramatist.

What is said in this play expresses the general formula for the later romances as well. In *The Tempest*, for example, certain illusions, such as Ariel's songs and the wedding masque, turn out to be the essential realities of the dramatic action; the *Realpolitik* of Antonio, his proposal to murder Alonso before he and Sebastian have any idea how they are to get off the island, is the kind of illusory pseudo-action that is symbolized by Ariel's harpy banquet, the meal spread out and snatched away. We are back to the Tantalus imagery of *Troilus and Cressida*, where the realities within the illusions are never quite grasped. But in *The Tempest* the audience is presented with an action in which reality is grasped through illusion. The climax of the illusion, the masque, is interrupted by Prospero with his great speech telling us that reality itself is simply an illusion that lasts a little longer.

In *A Midsummer Night's Dream* one very important character is the moon: the moon is referred to incessantly by all the characters, and lunar imagery comes in even where there is no direct reference to the moon, as in Theseus' 'the lunatic, the lover and the poet,' or Lysander's allusion to Demetrius as 'this spotted and inconstant man.' As an image of something she cannot possibly believe, Hermia speaks of the moon breaking through to the antipodes and joining the sun there, somewhat in the spirit of Lewis Carroll's walrus and carpenter poem. And yet in this play the daylight and the moonlight world do have some kind of equal and simultaneous validity: the dream world enters into and informs waking experience, though, as Bottom discovers, it is very difficult to reverse the process and reconstruct the dream. And so, as Puck says in the Epilogue, those in the audience who don't like the play can pretend that they have dreamed it. For those who are unable to pretend this, and know that they have seen it, there is a final act of reversal and recognition in the drama: the act in which the play passes from the stage into the minds of the audience.

'Lord, what fools these mortals be!' says Puck, as though he had nothing to do with making them behave foolishly. Actually, nobody in the play impresses us as a fool except Egeus, the invoker of law, and certainly Bottom, the only mortal who actually sees any of the fairies, is no fool, whatever Puck may say. The wood is unmistakably a wood of Eros: Cupid's darts and magic potions are all about us, and people behave very strangely under erotic influence. As Plato had said so many centuries previously, Eros can never be clearly separated from madness, and madness, though a different thing from folly, often appears as folly in the waking world. Hermia coaxes Lysander to sleep a little further from her: this is no doubt a very proper way for a young lady to behave who is spending a night in the woods with her lover, but her doing this is the cause of Puck's mistake. The prototype of Bottom, Lucius in Apuleius, is also transformed into an ass, and his life in that form is mostly one of misery; yet it is during his metamorphosis that Lucius hears the wonderful story of the separating and reunion of Love and the Soul, of Cupid and Psyche. Bottom himself, back in human shape, has lost his Titania, and will never see her again, but something has happened to him in the mean time infinitely far above his normal experience as Bottom the weaver.

In Classical mythology, to which *A Midsummer Night's Dream* owes a great deal, the moon is female, and is a part of what Robert Graves calls the Triple Will, being also the virgin huntress Diana (one of whose names in Ovid is Titania) on earth and Hecate or Persephone in the lower world: Puck speaks of 'triple Hecate's team.' It might be possible, then, to think that the fairy world represents a female principle in the play which is eventually subordinated to a male ascendancy associated with daylight. In the background is the unseen little boy who moves from female to male company as Oberon simultaneously asserts his authority over Titania; in the foreground is Theseus' marriage to a conquered Amazon. But this seems wrong, and out of key with the general tonality of the play. Theseus' marriage will at least end his unsavoury reputation as a treacherous lover, glanced at by Oberon, and the most explicit symbol of male domination, Egeus' claim to dispose of Hermia as he wishes, is precisely what is being eliminated by the total action. The fairy wood is a wood of Eros as well as of Venus and Diana, and both sexes are equally active principles in both worlds.

The relation of the two worlds is turned inside out in *Romeo and Juliet*, which is probably near to *A Midsummer Night's Dream* in date. In this play the character that makes the most impressively described entrances is the sun, which ushers in days when the blood as well as the temperature is hot and quarrelling families are abroad. Here the stories of Pyramus and Thisbe and the *Knight's Tale* are acted out in grisly earnest (the *Knight's Tale* theme is embryonic only, but the ghost of it appears in the rivalry of Paris for Juliet). *Romeo and Juliet* is uniquely a tragedy without villains, for even Tybalt is a man of honour according to his own lights, and is probably no more belligerent than Mercutio in any case. The other characters seem to be rather decent and well-meaning people: how do we get six deaths out of their interactions? For a common-sense, daylight explanation we need only the family feud, but Romeo (and the Prologue) ascribes the tragedy to malignant stars as well. In the dialogue, the fairy world of night, erotic feelings, and wish-fulfilment dreams has shrunk to Mercutio's account of Queen Mab. Yet the dreams Queen Mab inspires condition one's action when awake as well, and in the setting of *Romeo and Juliet* her influence is baleful, reminding us of what the lives of the four lovers in *A Midsummer Night's Dream* would have been if their fates had been left entirely to Puck. So Romeo is perhaps not wholly wrong in ascribing some of the disaster at least to a dark and mysterious world that seems pure illusion and yet somehow transforms what we call reality.

The traditional Christian explanation of reality and illusion is that God created a real and perfect world, and that man fell out of it into his present world, which is subject to the illusions generated by sin and death. The only progress toward reality that man is capable of is the progress from this world up toward the original world that was intended to be his home. This is a purgatorial ascent, the means being obedience to law, virtue, morality, and the sacraments of religion. Yet the goal of the journey, which is man's regaining of his own moral reality, appears as an illusion at first, because its original context of paradise or the Garden of Eden has disappeared. Spenser thus calls his world of moral realization 'Faerie.' Obviously the direction of man's regeneration has close similarities with the reversal of Aeneas' journey in the lower world and that fact, along with the Fourth Eclogue, does much to account for Virgil's later reputation as practically an honorary Christian.

Hence the structure of Christian doctrine in Shakespeare's day envisaged a conception of 'nature' on two levels. On the lower level was the 'fallen' world we are born in, to which animals and plants seem reasonably well adjusted, but from which man is or ought to be alienated. Man is to turn away from this level of nature and seek in his institutions a kind of discipline that will help to raise him to a higher and specifically human level of nature. It is 'natural' for man, though not for an animal, to wear clothes, to live under social discipline, to feel moral obligations, to accept the necessity of law. Even chastity and celibacy in sex can be 'natural' to man on this level of nature.

Nature on this higher human level is much the same thing as art, the state of art being also the state of human nature. Such a nature is primarily what is called *natura naturata*, nature as a structure or system, and is founded on the horror of idolatry which inspired so much of early Christianity and of Judaism before it. Idolatry means an absorption into a 'fallen' nature and an adoration of whatever is numinous in that nature. Christian teaching says that while fallen nature reflects much of the glory and wisdom of the original creation, it is not numinous: all the gods discovered in it are devils. The greatest of all these potential idols, strictly speaking, is the Eros that is founded in our own sexual impulses, and is consequently our central link with fallen nature.

Thus in *Paradise Lost* Adam and Eve are placed in the original providential form of the world. After the serpent has persuaded Eve to transgress the commandment about eating the forbidden fruit, Eve comes to Adam as a spirit of fallen nature, now a very dangerous idol. Adam yields to her urging to eat of the same fruit, because he would rather die with Eve than live without her. We are expected to sympathize with Adam, because Adam's fall is also ours, and in his situation we should have done the same thing. But still he falls from a world of reality which God had provided for him to a world of illusion, and his sexual relations with Eve sink from love to lust. Under God's guidance, however, Adam finds that there is a solid bottom of reality to this illusory world, and he reaches it when he and Eve join hands as they walk out of their garden into a lower world. The joining of hands is the beginning of a human community that struggles all through history to regain its lost heritage; and the love in it is inspired by compassion and not by passion.

This construct of two levels of nature endured long past Shakespeare's day into the eighteenth century, when it began to fall to pieces. It lasted so long because it was part of an ideological structure of authority. The first stirrings of political, and, later, economic and technological revolution weakened it, and the Romantic movement brought in a new ideology assuming that man was first of all a product of nature, whether fallen or not, a *natura naturans* from which he derived all his powers, including his intelligence. Romanticism was part of the general modern tendency to try to get past thinking in terms of a simple opposition of reality and illusion. In the previous century Vico, though without much influence in his time, had laid down the principle of *verum factum*, that man understands only what he has made. Or, perhaps more accurately, man understands reality only through the medium of some fiction that he has created, whether a verbal or a mathematical fiction. Any sort of reality that lies beyond or outside such human fictions is pure alienation, and inaccessible to us. Hence literature also exerts its authority, and communicates what truths it possesses, only through what Wallace Stevens calls a supreme fiction, a structure that has been made in the full knowledge that it is a fiction.

The Romantic construct gave a central importance to Eros, as the source not merely of love but of creative power as well. This aspect of Romanticism is directly descended from the stress that poets, and only poets, placed on Eros from medieval times through all the intervening centuries. The Romantics restated what had always been a central vision of poetry, and we can find in Shakespeare, especially in the more romantic comedies, the same conception of an illusion that turns into created reality through the influence of love. What the waking world calls folly or madness maybe dramatically superior to what it calls reality, as with Florizel's determination to remain faithful to Perdita:

> If my reason
> Will thereto be obedient, I have reason;
> If not, my senses, better pleased with madness,
> Do bid it welcome.

In observed reality we try to separate what is illusory in our perception, as we try to separate our sense that the earth is flat and fixed from what other observations tell us. In created reality there can be no exclusion of the illusory, which is the kernel of the supreme fiction superior to reality.

We have wandered from the play with which we began this discussion, the third 'problem comedy' of *Troilus and Cressida*, but we suggested the reason for doing so at the beginning. *Troilus and Cressida*, the earliest in its chronological setting of any Shakespeare play, is a play about the beginning of history, and shows us how man acquires the sense of illusory reality that the playwright tries to reverse into real illusion. It represents one extreme of Shakespeare's dramatic spectrum, as the more romantic comedies, including the four romances, represent the other. The Trojan war has set up its version of reality, which is a machinery of causation, a pseudo-fatality in which the Trojans must go on fighting to keep Helen. Troilus must therefore agree to Cressida's going to her father in the Greek camp (we note in passing the reversal of the normal comic movement of the heroine from father to lover) in order to maintain the fiction about Helen that he had defended himself. Cressida may be 'faithless,' but fidelity would be impossibly quixotic in the world she is in, a world where heroism degenerates into brutality and love itself is reduced to another kind of mechanical stimulus, as Thersites points out with so much relish. When at the end of the play Pandarus shrivels into a contemporary London pimp, professionally concerned with the spreading of syphilis, there is very little sense of shock or incongruity: we have already realized that this play is about us, if not about the aspect of us that we want to put on exhibition.

It is by a final irony of language that we call the portrayal of such a world 'disillusioned,' and associate the term pejoratively with a weary pessimism. Being disillusioned with a world like that is the starting point of any genuine myth of deliverance. We take our first step towards such disillusionment when we realize that the basis of consciousness in such a world is the perception of time and space as Ulysses expounds them. Thinking in terms of time and space, however, though familiar to us, is post-Newtonian rather than Shakespearean: in Shakespeare's day what we call space was usually expressed as place, or space-*there*. The world of degree, where everything has its natural place, or what Chaucer calls its 'kindly stead,' is a discontinuous conception of space: only wisdom and prudence seek for the natural place and try to stay in it; the arrogance and pride of the vast majority try to get above it and end by falling below it. Time for Ulysses is also discontinuous: it is time-*then*, a series of moments very loosely connected by memory or sustained attention, its main linking force being the automatic one of repetition.

At the other extreme in Shakespeare time and place have a creative instead of a destructive role. We have mentioned the curious double recognition in the romances, where older people heal breaches in their pasts by the power of love in a context of art, and younger people go out into a new life by the power of love in a context of nature. The main emphasis is on the former. In *Pericles* the marriage of Marina and Lysimachus is subordinated to the reunion of Pericles with his wife and daughter. In *Cymbeline* there is the same past-future double recognition, as Cymbeline's lost sons are restored to him and provide an heir for the future, while Posthumus' lost parents reappear in a dream. But again the emphasis falls on the healing up of the past, and there is no new marriage at the end at all. In *The Winter's Tale* Time is not only the chorus of the play but seems in some mysterious way to be an arranger of the action, or what we have called a deputy dramatist: the subtitle of Green's *Pandosto* is 'The Triumph of Time.' In *The Tempest*, even the title (*tempestas*, meaning time as well as tempest) suggests the near-obsession with time that seems to affect everyone in the play, the centre of it being Prospero's vast magical experiment, which, like all works performed by magic, depends on timing of the most precise kind.

Of all the arts linked with creative time, music has a special place as pre-eminently the art of time, an association that runs all through Shakespeare, a familiar example being Richard ii's prison speech. But because of its associations with the harmony of the spheres and cosmic order, music has no less intimate a link with conceptions of degree and natural place. Unnatural acts, such as rebellion, are linked with discord, as Pericles remarks of the incestuous daughter of Antiochus:

> But being played upon before your time,
> Hell only danceth at so harsh a chime.

There is a curious and sometimes rather off-putting snobbery in the romances: Perdita can remain with Florizel only because she is a real princess; Guiderius, who kills the oaf Cloten in *Cymbeline*, is released from a death sentence only because he is 'better than the man he slew,' i.e., superior in social rank; Antonio and Sebastian retain their social superiority to Stephano and Trinculo at the end of *The Tempest* in spite of their melancholy moral performance. Such themes seem to be structurally connected with the emphasis on the restoration of the rightful past.

In *The Tempest* particularly we see how the illusions of Ariel gradually transform the kind of life represented by the shoddy realism of Antonio into a superior kind of reality. Antonio's *Realpolitik* echoes Achilles in *Troilus and Cressida*, who satisfies one of Ulysses' concerns for degree and place by returning to the Greek army, but then pulls down Hector, who is far above him in any conception of 'degree' that would make sense at all, by a combination of treachery and ferocity. The supreme fiction of *The*

Tempest is the wedding masque, an illusion within an illusion, where the goddesses of heaven, earth, and the rainbow provide a vision of paradise that prompts Ferdinand to say, echoing Peter in the Transfiguration, 'Let me live here ever.' But Prospero speaks and interrupts the masque, and there follows a speech where we are back in the world of a time that devours and annihilates everything, even the great globe itself. Nevertheless, Ferdinand and Miranda have been given the masque as a wedding present, to be the emblem of their whole lives.

Prospero's epilogue suggests that the entire play is something similar for its audience:

> As you from crimes would pardoned be,
> Let your indulgence set me free.

The basis of the epilogue is the conventional appeal for applause: Prospero has done his work, renounced his magic, and exhausted his powers: it is now for the audience to respond. But Prospero's language is more serious than that: it makes practically a religious issue, echoing the Lord's Prayer, out of the reception of the play. Prospero himself, following Ariel, merely wants release and freedom; we are to go home and take with us only what he has given us. But even granting that the audience's recognition of the play is the final recognition, and the reversal of its direction into their minds the final reversal, still play and audience are two things, and the recognition still does not have the final quality of entering into and becoming one with the thing recognized. After we have applauded and set Prospero free, what do we do with ourselves?

I have said that when Shakespeare repeats something in a play it should be closely examined; but what should be examined even more closely are the totally pointless passages of filler which Shakespeare has stuck in merely to keep the characters talking.

There are no such passages, but there are some that look like that. In the first scene of Act Two of *The Tempest* we are introduced to the Court Party, where Sebastian, an obvious weakling, has reacted to shipwreck by a state of giggling hysteria. Antonio falls in with his mood and encourages it, because he knows what he wants to do with Sebastian later. Gonzalo has asserted with great confidence that Tunis was the ancient Carthage: it was not, but the point of saying so is to indicate that *The Tempest* is partly modelled on the underworld descent of Aeneas in Book VI of the *Aeneid*. Antonio and Sebastian make fun of his solecism, and Antonio says:

ANTONIO   What impossible matter will he make easy next?
SEBASTIAN   I think he will carry this island home in his pocket, and give it his son for an apple.
ANTONIO   And, sowing the kernels of it in the sea, bring forth more islands.

We hardly expect Antonio, of all people, to be the one to tell us what we should be doing with the experience of seeing *The Tempest*. And yet Shakespeare, who has a knack of making impossible matters easy, seems to be suggesting, however indirectly, that this is also what we can do: take the island home with us as we would an apple, and make it for us and for our children a source of further islands in the sea. The last reversal of the action into our minds brings about the last recognition, the incorporating of the play into our own creative lives and traditions. In ordinary experience action, energy, and reality are the phenomena of a life proceeding towards death. The portrayal of the reversal of these things in dramatic and other literature will not make us immortal, but it will give our imaginations a depth and a perspective that can take in other possibilities, chiefly the possibility of a more intense mode of living. Prospero the magician claims to have raised the dead; Prospero the dramatist practises a more credible and more useful art, the art of waking up what is dead or sleeping within us, like Hermione stirring within Julio Romano's statue and responding to Paulina's challenge of 'Be stone no more.'